D1612507

ALL
VALIANT
DUST

ALL
VALIANT
DUST

AN IRISHMAN ABROAD

PETER ROSS

THE LILLIPUT PRESS

First published in 1992 by
THE LILLIPUT PRESS LTD
4 Rosemount Terrace, Arbour Hill,
Dublin 7, Ireland

A CIP record for this
title is available from
The British Library.

ISBN 0 946640 89 0

Jacket design by The Graphiconies (Bortoli)
Set in 10 on 12 Palatino by
mermaid turbulence
on an Apple Macintosh
Printed in Dublin by
Colour Books Ltd of Baldoyle

All valiant dust that builds on dust,
And guarding, calls not thee to guard,
For frantic boast and foolish word –
Thy mercy on thy People, Lord!

'Recessional'
Rudyard Kipling

FOREWORD

In 1953 Jack Sweetman, who played rugby for Old Wesley and had had a final trial for Ireland, asked me to coach boxing in Brook House School. As I got out of the Law Library shortly after four, it would be great if I could come along and put the mites through their paces. Jack was soon to move on to Headfort School, where he became a legendary figure. After he left I continued to coach at Brook House, which was how I came to know Peter Ross, the headmaster there. Peter was a small man, well below average height, and it seemed incredible to me that he should have been a first-class soccer player at Repton and awarded the Military Cross at El Alamein. A born schoolmaster, he inspired boys to fulfil their physical and mental potential. At football matches he would run up and down the sidelines like a terrier, yelling with the enthusiasm of a thirteen-year-old, 'Come on, Brook House!' Once he discovered that the oval ball game was the only one played in Irish prep schools, he became as knowledgeable and fanatical about it as he had been about soccer.

A condition under which I had agreed to coach boxing at Brook House was that I should not be paid a salary. I would like to think that this scruple was born out of a strict loyalty to the Corinthian code, but there may have been at the back of my mind the fear that an insolent jack-in-office would at some future date demand the return of the sports trophies I had won, on the grounds that I forfeited my amateur status by coaching for financial reward. However, though I received neither silver nor gold for my efforts, I was rewarded in kind.

One of the teachers at the school was the writer Monk Gibbon, and it was through Peter that I began a thirty-year friendship with Monk, or Bill, as he was known to his friends.

Peter had a genuine love of literature and was an admirer of
Gibbon's work, and conversations over tea, after I had taught
the boys the value of a straight left and, more importantly, how
to avoid that of their opponents, would be stimulating, as talk
of books and poetry flowed back and forth. Bill, like Peter, was
an excellent sportsman, a six handicap at golf, and a crack
hockey player. The other prep schools in Dublin at that time,
Aravon and Castle Park, were long established, and it took an
enormous amount of energy and organization on Peter's part
to keep Brook House going. But it grew rapidly, after ten years
moving from Clonskeagh to Ashtown Park in Monkstown, and
then to Bray. The school was founded in 1952, by 1955 there
were fifty boys, and at its height numbers rose to 190.

In mid-career Peter had a serious cardiac illness which
would have meant retirement for most. But it didn't seem to
take a feather out of him; he even increased his work-load.
Fortunately he had an ideal partner to assist him – his wife,
Paddy. When I first came to Brook House I was dazzled, as
was everyone else, by this lovely-looking girl – the perfect
English Rose, who rivalled in looks the current stars of the
British screen revival, Deborah Kerr, Glynis Johns and Greer
Garson. Sunny-tempered and full of laughter, Paddy seemed
to do everything: run the house-keeping, supervise the dining-
room, help with the accounts, remaining through it all a
seraphic figure who represented in this all-male school the
female psyche which was part of the boys' lives at home.

Peter was born during a bridging period in the evolution of
Irish society, when Ireland was part of the United Kingdom,
but was to spend most of his life in a country which had
become self-governing. It was an era when the Anglo-Irish
exerted themselves in establishing an identity: Yeats, AE, Lady
Gregory, Synge and Douglas Hyde had probed the imagination of their class, and striven to recognize the Irish side of
their personalities. Those who came after them were helped by
that great creative burst at the turn of the century further to
pursue and explore the nature of the identity of their class as
Irishmen. We get a glimpse of this in the Introduction to *All
Valiant Dust* when Peter recalls an argument with a bullying
history master at Repton who had vilified Ireland. Even when
he was thousands of miles away, memories of home were

always flitting through his mind. In the desert the night before the battle of El Alamein he would remember sailing in Donegal Bay with a friend the day war was declared. The desert in winter, 'in that moment of semi-darkness when the sun sank behind the horizon', induced in him nostalgic memories of an Irish bog.

I think one episode here shows as tellingly as anything I have ever read the identity that can be forged between Irishmen of different backgrounds when they are outside their own country. The Catholic chaplain in his battalion, who he calls Father Joyce, was from the West of Ireland. The other officers knew that Father Joyce had a weakness – he cheated at cards. These officers would make Peter furious by adding condescendingly, 'You see, he's Irish.'

Then one day there was a German air attack and Peter lay flat on the ground with his company unable to rescue a nearby anti-aircraft gun crew who had been bombed and some of whom were seriously injured.

Suddenly, as another wave of bombers manoeuvred into the sun, a staff car moved out towards the stricken gun crew.

'Get back, you idiot!' someone shouted.

The car lurched and stopped, a jagged hole torn in its side. Out of it stepped a man, very deliberately, as though nothing extraordinary were happening. It was Father Joyce, the sleeves of his white shirt rolled above his elbows. He walked purposefully towards the wounded men. Bombs were bursting all around him, and bullets splintering the shale. But on he went. He bound up wounds; he gave spiritual comfort where he could not otherwise help. He never faltered, never even ducked when the bombs landed near him.

Later on I saw him, armed with a spade and a pick, digging graves through that ungiving surface.

That evening he arrived late for the game of cards, because he was writing letters to the relatives of the dead and wounded.

Bravery in battle is sometimes a matter of impulse caused by fear, an adrenalin-driven act to hide a greater fear, a fear of death through inaction, or even the fear of being thought afraid.

But Father Joyce's actions were not a matter of impulse. They were deliberate, they were continuous, aimed at helping men in mortal danger. There were no heroics for Father Joyce, no 'going over the top', rifle in hand, inspired by the thrill of combat. Had there been no war, and had I known him only in peace-time, I would probably have written him off as a petty buffoon. How many acts of courage and devotion are curtained off behind apparently uneventful lives?

Which was the real Father Joyce – the man who cheated at cards to win a few pence, or the man who risked his life so fearlessly to help those soldiers? It is an imponderable question, since it suggests that the complexity of human motives and feelings can be expressed in terms of black and white. I know that Father Joyce didn't cheat for the money, which could mean nothing to him. It may have been an act, a 'playing Irish' to amuse his fellow officers, or even a fling of contempt and defiance at their assumption of superiority.

Peter Ross's war started when he joined the 3rd Battalion of the Royal Tank Regiment as a second lieutenant under the command of the much-decorated General Robert Crisp, the famous South African Test cricketer.

Some time later, on 23 October 1942, Peter found himself pitched into the battle of El Alamein, where he was badly wounded during a rescue operation from a burning tank. Even in its reserved military prose, the citation describing the action – for which he was awarded the MC and promoted to captain – conveys his exceptional courage.

On 29th October, 1942, a Crusader Tank was knocked out by anti-tank gunfire. Three members of the crew were badly burnt.

2/Lt. Ross unhesitatingly took up his Scout Car to the burning tank which was within a few hundred yards of enemy M.G. and anti-tank gun positions. In his Scout Car he ferried the wounded men back to a second Crusader under heavy M.G. and a tk fire.

2/Lt. Ross then travelled with the wounded men on the back of the second Crusader until it was hit and set alight. The clothes of all the men on the back and in the Crusader caught fire.

2/Lt. Ross beat out the flames with his bare hands and helped the wounded to the safety of slit trenches nearby.

All this time the party was under very heavy M.G. and a tk gunfire.

2/Lt. Ross did not rest or attempt to protect himself until the last wounded man was safely evacuated. He suffered severe burns and shock. His very gallant action saved many valuable lives.

Peter wrote to his parents:

For some mysterious reason I have been awarded a decoration. Can't think why. I'm happy about it for one reason – it is for helping to save lives, not to take them.

One might think of this as false modesty. But I don't think it is. He remained throughout the war and, indeed, throughout his life, puzzled by the whole strange business of killing, and sceptical about the value of war: 'The result was glorious but the actual battle wasn't. Like all battles, it was hideous.'

Some of the best insights into the nature of war have come from writers depicting it from the point of view of non-combatants and peripheral dodgers, like O'Casey in *Juno and the Paycock* and Shakespeare with Pistol Bardolph and the Fat Knight in the Henrys. In *All Valiant Dust* the writer is a participant, but writing with an imaginative eye in finely balanced prose, he manages to involve us in the mayhem of the battlefield and yet retain something of the detachment of the commentator. Perhaps he was in a position to do this because of the ambivalent element in the Anglo-Irish personality. Like Denis Johnston, another Irishman involved in the El Alamein preparations, Peter Ross could stand apart, not indulging himself in a hatred of the enemy understandable in the English and French, who had already faced the Germans in a ferocious war, and still held the memory of the slaughtered dead.

Peter was then lucky to find a niche with another hero of his, General 'Pete' Pyman DSO, who had commanded at El Alamein and was now chief of staff on the 30 Corps. As his 'Personal Assistant', Peter was present at the planning headquarters for the D-Day landings. He was involved in the first day of the invasion at Gold Beach and the subsequent breakout from Normandy. After the liberation of Brussels, the corps headquarters set up in a nunnery near Nijmegen, where they remained during the disastrous Arnhem landings. Later, as an instructor at Sandhurst, Peter was commissioned to write a history of the academy during the war.

It was a coincidence that the only battle of which I have any knowledge whatsoever should be El Alamein. This unlikely mental baggage was taken aboard when I was retained to act as counsel for General Auchinleck's chief of staff, General Eric Dorman-Smith, in a libel action involving the conduct of the Alamein campaign. It required me to undertake a detailed study of the position of the two armies and the strategic plans which led to the final victory. Carrying out prolonged interviews with Captain Basil Liddell Hart, the well-known strategist (said to be the inventor of modern tank warfare), Corelli Barnett and others, as well as my own documentary research, I constructed a mental picture of the major events. The battle of Alam Halfa in July 1942 was generally referred to as 'First

Alamein' and the one beginning on 23 October, commanded by General Bernard Montgomery, as 'Second Alamein'. Peter Ross regarded the latter, which resulted in the rout of Rommel's forces, as the *real* battle of El Alamein. We had much genial debate on the subject and I was pleased to see that Peter pays generous tribute here to General Auchinleck (and, implicitly, to Dorman-Smith) for the holding operation at the Alamein redoubt, which prepared the ground for Montgomery's success.

Peter did not live to see his memoir appear in print. Talking to him a few days before he died, I told him how delighted I was to learn that it was to be published in the near future, and thought I detected a note of schoolboy glee in his voice before he put down the receiver. He'd brought it off again. A few days later I learnt that his heart had finally given in, and that we would talk no more.

Ulick O'Connor
Dublin, May 1992

PREFACE

My memories of the war years are mostly of moments of drama, excitement, humour, fear and pain. Rejected are the times between battles and leaves, times that were grey with the desolation of years lost, and the drab anticipation that war would never end.

Those six years, 1939 to 1945, were the richest in the lives of many who survived. Whatever damage was done to mind or body by the frustrations of service life, or in battle or in air raid, we lived with an intensity quickened by the expectation of death. We came out of the war feeling spuriously heroic, a little hysterical, a little self-conscious in our well-worn uniforms decorated with ribbons, missing the thrills, the drama, the camaraderie. And in the following years of civilian life we tended to forget that we had once been different, resigned – if not dedicated – to destroying an evil that defiled all Europe and beyond.

Nevertheless I often wondered why men allow themselves to be committed to battle, knowing they face the likelihood of immediate death or an excruciating wound. Where is that natural fear which protects us from physical hurt? What possible ideal can give death precedence over life?

My late friend, the poet and writer Monk Gibbon, asked a similar question in *Inglorious Soldier*:

The more we reverence life the harder it becomes to accept fortuitous and unnecessary death. And yet millions of men do so without complaint. Is it because they feel themselves to have been caught in a web of destiny from which there is no escape? Or have they surrendered to a collective madness which has taken possession of almost all, and which makes them willing victims? Or do they undervalue life and so cast it the more easily aside? Or have they no choice? I am amazed at the unprotesting acceptance of the inevitable by these attitudes.

Before El Alamein, my first battle, I suffered devastating fear, but once it started I was consumed by that 'collective madness'. I seemed to be taken over by a force deriving from the battle itself, its mesmerizing din and majestic violence. There was a compulsion, an ecstasy, a kind of religious fervour, and an arrogant conviction of immunity from death or wounds. And that collective madness became a sense of community, of sharing an unfamiliar, outrageous, inescapable danger.

INTRODUCTION

Beginnings – An Anglo-Irish Childhood

India during the Great War was no place for white babies. I was born of Irish parents in the hills of what is now Pakistan at the end of July 1914.

My father worked in the Public Works Department, which provided, among other benefits, the canals that even today bring life to many arid areas of the subcontinent.

At the time, infants were brought 'home' as soon as possible because of the adverse effects of Indian food and climate. In my case, however, and in that of my younger brother Frank, this was impossible because all civilian shipping had been requisitioned. I was five days old when the Great War started.

Although still almost a baby when at last we left India, I have some misty memories: the river flowing past our bungalow at Jhelum, silver-grey, with a constant whispering sound; the jackals howling at night, and my mother coming to clasp me in case I was frightened, which of course I pretended to be so she would stay, her warmth comforting as I snuggled against her breast; the tall bearer, Aziz, who moved so silently that he could be standing behind you for some time before you knew he was there, and whose perpetually sorrowful expression earned him the nickname 'Joy-and-Laughter'; and Abdul, the cook, who made such wonderful chapattis, and who never forgot, even when I was at Repton, to make a cake for my birthday. This used to arrive in a tall grey tin, soldered at the edges, and when it was opened there escaped a rich fruit-laden smell. Alcohol was used as a preservative, and my friends and I liked to think it made us drunk.

There was one strange association which remained latent until I was twenty-one. My father had arranged for me to miss the summer term at Trinity College, Dublin so that I could visit him in India. As we motored northwards from Bombay I became aware of a strange, pungent, not unpleasant smell.

'Are we anywhere near Jhelum?'

'About a quarter of a mile. Why on earth do you ask?'

'Because of that smell. It reminds me of when I was a baby. Is it the timber drying out on the bank of the river?'

And into my mind came a vision of the grey beams that had been floated down from the mountains, shaped into railway sleepers and then piled in neat squares on the bank.

When the war ended we 'came home' by the famous P&O line to England, and then on to Ireland. My parents returned to India for another three-year stint before their next leave, and my brother and I lived with our paternal grandparents in Fitzwilliam Street in Dublin. The vicious civil war which was to tear Ireland apart was not far in the future. Being six years old I had no idea of the issues at stake. There were, though, moments of excitement, such as when our grandfather, known as Grampy, came into the bedroom and moved our beds so that we could not be hit by random snipers. And there was one evening of sheer terror. We had been put to bed when Grampy came up to say goodnight, adding that we were not to be frightened; some soldiers were searching the houses in the area for weapons and would be coming upstairs in a few minutes.

Now, my passion at that time was Meccano. By screwing together some of the longer pieces of metal I had produced a rather fine outline of a rifle. What was I to do? If the soldiers found it what would *they* do? Imprison me? Or worse, shoot me? In terror I jumped out of bed, seized the terrible piece, pushed it under the blanket and lay down on top of it.

The door opened and two soldiers in green uniform came in. They were very polite to our nurse.

'I don't suppose these little soldiers have any guns hidden away!'

Soldiers! For a moment of horror I thought they were going to start a search, but with a cheerful goodnight they left. Next morning I hastily unscrewed that fearsome weapon.

One night we were wakened by a series of tremendous explosions. Our nursery was on the top floor and we could see, across the roofs of the houses opposite, the sky lit up by an angry blood-red blaze. It was early morning, before dawn, on 28 June

1922. Free State forces using field guns borrowed from the British had bombarded the Four Courts and set them on fire.

In time I was sent to a kindergarten in Mespil Road, run by a stern but lovable lady called Miss Morse. My nurse used to accompany me along the few hundred yards between the school and Fitzwilliam Street. One day as we crossed Baggot Street Bridge a lorry filled with troops swerved in front of us and proceeded up Wilton Terrace at speed. There was an explosion and we saw it rise crazily into the air, blown sideways and upwards by the blast of the mine. My nurse dragged me into a doorway, where we stayed until she was sure it was safe to go on.

When I was nine I was sent to a small preparatory school in Kent. It was customary in those days that people of our background and tradition should be educated in England rather than in Ireland. This particular school was renowned for its discipline, which was probably why my father chose it. He admired the headmaster, Major Peters, who had been decorated for gallantry in Flanders, and who ran his school on regimental lines. Right was right, wrong was wrong, orders were orders, and there was no such thing as a mitigating circumstance. For every crime there was an appropriate punishment.

'You, boy, why aren't you writing?'

'Please, Sir, my pencil needs sharpening.'

'Your pencil needs sharpening, does it? It is your duty to be prepared for class. What do you suppose would happen to a soldier going into battle with no ammunition for his rifle, eh? He'd be shot. He'd be shot. Hold out your hand.' Excruciating pain.

Another scene. I can hear again the indignant treble voices.

'It was *your* fault anyway.'

'No it wasn't, *you* started talking – '

'No I didn't, I only laughed.'

'Why should we *all* be kept in just because you and Jimmy were – '

'Shut up! – the Hun's coming!'

Twenty heads bend over twenty sheets of paper. Twenty cramped hands push pens or pencils along the faint blue lines: I must not talk after lights out I must not talk after lights out I must not . . .

'Who vos talkink now?'

No answer. Some look up, some go on writing.

'Who vos talkink now, I say!'

Blond, blue-eyed, athletic. The dimple-cleft chin slightly raised, rectangular brow marble-white; alert suspicious eyes flickering snake-like along the desks, the head not moving. Why did the Major have a German on his staff? He'd been shooting Germans not so long ago himself and everyone knew why, because of the dreadful atrocities they committed . . .

On Parents' Day Müller had flashed his smile at my mother.

'What a handsome young man,' she said, 'he must be *very* nice, he looks *so* kind. What's his name?'

'The Hun and he's a bully.'

'I *can't* believe it. Another ice, dear?'

If only she could see him now!

'Vell! so nobody vos talkink! I vos hearing vot vos not there, nein? You, you, you – und you – go down to the gym.'

'But, Sir – '

The words die on my tongue as I see the flickering at the corner of his eyes, the sudden tightening of the lips.

' – Yes, Sir.'

'You vill change to games togs first. You haf thirty seconds.'

Now he stands in the open doorway of the gym. We are lined up, the four of us, a few yards away, facing him.

'About turn! Hips firm – on der toes rise – double-knee bend – arms bend – arms upvard stretch. Now you vill stay still, you vill not move till I come back.'

One minute, two minutes. Pain creeps up from my shoulders to my arms. I cannot keep them up any longer. They are quivering now. And my legs have gone to sleep and I'm beginning to fall.

'Jimmy,' I whisper to my friend.

'It's all right,' says Jimmy, 'the swine's forgotten us.'

Thankfully I let my arms flop down, and my legs give way. As I fall I hear a thump and a cry beside me. Jimmy lurches forward, the Hun propelling him with vicious kicks across the floor.

I scream at him.

'Shut up, you German bully, leave him alone!'

I scream again as he turns and strides towards me, his hands clenched and his lips drawn back, showing his teeth. I know he wants nothing but to hurt me with all his strength. I cover my eyes and cower to the floor, waiting for the blow.

It doesn't come. Suddenly there is silence. Müller is drawn up, rigid and white, staring past us. The muscles in his cheek are twitching. Cautiously I look round. The Major is standing in the door. He says nothing but looks at Müller through half-closed eyes. For a while they stare at each other. I forget the pain in my limbs as I wonder if Müller is going to hit him. What will happen if he does? It's unthinkable; headmasters are all-powerful, untouchable, unhittable. But Müller is stronger, younger and bigger.

Suddenly Müller moves. We hold our breath as he steps forward with a wooden action like a soldier on parade and marches, looking straight ahead, past the Major and out through the door. The Major is motionless, even when Müller seemed to start towards him. I knew now how brave the Major was, and he became an even stronger symbol in my mind of authority, aloof, fearless, calmly certain of instant obedience.

As for Müller, we never saw him again, and he was never spoken of. This was a relief, of course, but I could never forget that scene of victory and defeat. Sometimes I would identify myself with Müller, the bully humiliated, and sometimes with the Major, cold, ruthless, power personified.

My respect for the Major was now totally unquestioning, an ingenuous hero-worship. Later on I realized that this was based on fear, for he conditioned us into complete acceptance. Whatever Authority decreed, however absurd it might seem to our immature minds, *must* have some good purpose behind it. Rebellion, therefore, would be silly, leading to all sorts of evil which we were not old enough to understand, nor even to know of.

This submission to his will and personality, though wrapping me in a comfortable security at the time, resulted later in a shattering destruction of my self-esteem. It never occurred to me to rebel against his system because I could conceive of none other, but high spirits occasionally led me into trouble. After some schoolboy escapade he said to me, 'Of course, Ross, I should have expected nothing else, you're such a weak character.'

Because of my belief in his godlike omniscience the judgment stayed with me for many years, and I grew from an uninhibited bouncy child into a hesitating, self-doubting adolescent. Many years later when I became a headmaster myself I remembered the effect of this casually demoralizing remark and tried never to humiliate even the most repulsive of pupils; so perhaps a little good came of it.

When my parents returned on leave from India there was inevitably a gulf between us. Each thought of the other as they had been three years before. When I was twelve my mother tended to treat me according to the picture stored in her mind of the little nine-year-old she had last seen; and to me she was alien, not aware of the things that had happened to me since, suspicious of the development that separated me from her. At first I would resent being treated like a baby; and she, I think, felt that the infant whom she had loved and who had been so dependent on her no longer existed, but was replaced by a self-assertive creature with a life of its own, a life she could not possibly intrude on, nor even imagine.

As time went on, however, a new understanding would grow up between us. We shared jokes again; she could applaud my little successes, and comfort me in my failures. But just when this reached its fulfilment she would have to sail for India.

For another three years, my brother and I suffered makeshift holidays, sometimes spent in a hotel or guest-house near the school, sometimes with our grandparents in Ireland. They had moved out to De Vesci Terrace in Dún Laoghaire, or Kingstown as it was then called.

My grandfather, despite his small stature, was impressive in appearance. White-haired, with neatly cut moustache and imperial beard, and laughter-lines below his temples, he seemed to embody dignity and success. A partner in an engineering firm called Kaye Parry Ross, he did not, apparently, handle his financial affairs very ably. Furthermore, he was humiliatingly dominated by his second wife, Jane, a strait-laced symbol of all that was most tedious in the Victorian way of life. No mention was ever allowed of his first wife.

He was said to have been a gifted mathematician both at

school at Merchiston Castle in Scotland, and at university. When I was twelve he gave me the prize he had won at school for Maths, a magnificent leather-bound volume of Shakespeare's plays. I remember being surprised at the inscription: 'Presented to George Murray Ross, Second Prize for Mathematics, Class VI, Session 1869-70.' *Second* Prize? Why not *First* if he was so ... Also in my possession is a beautiful tiny little shield which looks like gold but isn't. This was a trophy of the Rifle Association of the Edinburgh Schools and was awarded to G.M. Ross in 1870.

I know that he went to France in May 1917 because I have the cigarette-case he was given 'By a Few Friends on his Departure', but I never discovered what part he played; he was certainly too old for a fighting role. The cigarette-case was an apt choice: he was a chain-smoker and in the end smoked himself to death, the saying in those days being that every cigarette was a nail in your coffin. One hopes his friends were unaware of the dangers their gift would add to those he was about to incur. His favourite was Wills 'Gold Flake'. In 1927 when the news of his death was given to me at school I suffered both emotional and physical torments, because I wanted to cry when I went to bed but couldn't as it would keep the other boys awake and I would be jeered at as a cry-baby, so strong was the stiff-upper-lip syndrome, even among children.

His wife, Jane, known for some mysterious reason as Alice, accepted as he did the social attitudes of their day with majestic conformity. The Empire, powerful and everlasting, provided a satisfying creed for the right sort of people. Gentlemen opened the door for ladies and did not swear in their presence; and, conveniently, children might be seen but not heard, even when, led by Nanny, they were allowed down for a short while from the nursery. I considered this a very unnatural rule. The difficulty arose because my brother was a delicate child who had to be treated with the greatest care, and, being intelligent, was disposed to make use of this. When he committed some misdemeanour, such as breaking a window, he quite brazenly attributed the blame to me. My grandparents, to whom he was a little god, believed him implicitly and, despite my remonstrations, I would be sent to bed early with strict

orders not to keep the light on. It is to these incarcerations that
I owe my love of literature. Burrowing under the bedclothes to
avoid discovery, I used a small torch to read. In these unlikely
circumstances I read many of Shakespeare's plays in the edition
my grandfather had given me, as well as 'The Bab Ballads' and
Kipling's 'Barrackroom Ballads', learning many passages by
heart.

Although my brother and I called ourselves Irish it was with
carefully defined reservations. In fact we were Anglo-Irish,
which at that time meant more Anglo than Irish, and felt
'foreign' in both countries. This, coupled with our having no
home, led to a sense of rootlessness and alienation. We had no
sentimental attachments such as exist in families whose children grow up in a house they come to know as home.

And although in the holidays we lived in Ireland our
traditions were English. Naturally we absorbed the traditions
of our grandparents, who looked upon the Irish as if they were
'natives' of some backward colony – 'My dear, they would
never be able to govern themselves.' Everything British, then,
was superior, so we were sent to English schools. Trinity
College, Dublin, however, was different. Founded in 1592 by
charter of Queen Elizabeth I it was an Anglican university,
second in standing only to Oxbridge. Since my grandfather
and my father had been there it was in the order of events that
this should be the aim of both my brother and myself.

When I went to Repton I began to think rather differently, if
not very clearly, about Ireland. I read Bernard Shaw, W.B. Yeats,
Synge, and minor poets such as Eva Gore-Booth. Through them
I began to be aware of some of the tragedy of Irish history, but
I had no guide and was still steeped in the traditions of the
British divine right to rule; and of that figure of fun, the stage
Irishman.

Our history master, H.J. Snape, who owned a magnificent
mastiff dog which followed him about everywhere, and who
himself typified the British bulldog, only once in a two-year
course referred to Ireland. He described its inhabitants as
'vermin, absolute vermin – hamstring their horses!' I was aged
fifteen and very much in awe of this imposing tyrant, but my
pride was touched and I stood up and said, 'Sir, I resent that!'

'What's your name?'

'Ross, Sir.'

'You're Scotch, sit down!'

The Irish were cowards, he went on. During the time of the Black and Tans they used to shoot from behind hedges instead of coming out and fighting manfully face to face. Unfortunately, my knowledge of Irish history being then nil, I could not counter this, but it did occur to me that it was common sense not to try to fight on equal terms with a stronger and better-equipped enemy. However, such was Snape's conviction of British rightness, even of British righteousness, that anyone who opposed his view was a traitor.

I was lucky in that I had an above-average facility for playing soccer. Repton being one of the great soccer schools I gained kudos and confidence by getting on the First XI whilst still a fag – which was considered by some a most impertinent, even subversive, act; typically Irish, in fact. In my first year on the team we beat all other schools. In my second year the pattern was the same until the last match. We were playing Shrewsbury at home on that beautiful pitch lying between the ancient Garth, the Chapter House and the open countryside. We had no doubts about the result.

Initially all went the accustomed way. At half-time we were leading 4-0. Then our goalkeeper was concussed and carried off, followed by one of our backs with a broken leg. In those days there were no substitutions, so nine of us now faced the full Shrewsbury team. It wasn't long before they scored. Five minutes later it was 4-2, then 4-3; with ten minutes to go 4 all. It was a classic situation. Could we hold out? Unlike brave Horatius keeping the bridge we did not face 30,000 foes before, and the broad flood behind, but it felt like it. Pushing exhausted limbs to their limit we strove, this time like brave Horatius, constant still in mind. To lose was unthinkable, to win impossible. So we packed the goal and fought. My place was right-half, the left-half being Pyman, a boy my own age and in my house. To us and the centre-half fell the major defensive role. At last the whistle went, and we remained undefeated for another year.

The first class next day was History. Snape was a few minutes late. He strode in like the officer in charge of a firing-squad.

'Ross! Pyman! Stand up!'

Oh God, here it comes. He's going to test us on last night's prep, which we were both too worn out to do.

'Look at these boys, you others! – they've got guts! Guts! They played yesterday like the British soldiers at Mons!'

I was flabbergasted, so flabbergasted that the vision of the British soldiers playing soccer at Mons escaped me.

'They fought like tigers. A credit to the school. You may leave the classroom, you two, and do whatever you like. Well done!'

It was an unexpected tribute, and because of its source we knew it was sincere. So we slunk out, our classmates not daring to smirk, and we not sure whether to look like the soldiers playing soccer at Mons, or like tigers.

To me this match was a turning-point. Four apparently unrelated triumphs followed, doubtless influenced by my elevation to the team in a school where success at cricket or soccer was regarded as the acme of achievement. First, I was awarded my colours; second, I was released from fagging; third, I was promoted to sergeant in the OTC; and finally, I won the junior verse prize for what must have been the most outrageous piece of doggerel. This can hardly be ascribed to skill at soccer, but I never doubted that, because I was now a 'Teamer' (Repton slang for a member of a team who had won his colours), my contribution received more than sympathetic attention.

At first I hated Repton. There were several reasons for this, one of them being the wild Irishman image I was supposed to live up to. I discovered that acting the clown could become a permanent state, and had the wit to see that ultimately no one would take me seriously. Despite the loss of the cheap popularity I had enjoyed as a Paddy, I now began to rebel in earnest against some of the sillier aspects of public-school life. Many of the traditions were totally artificial and irrational.

For example, boys in the first year had to have all the buttons on their jackets done up. The following year you were allowed to have one button undone, and another the next year. Breaking this code led to dire punishment. The fagging system was antediluvian. You were a fag for your first two years, and subject to canings by a prefect if you did not satisfy his standards of slavery. To me these pettinesses added up to humiliation; I could not understand how my English peers

accepted it all. Many years later I realized it was this condi-
tioning to abject obedience that made them such competent
soldiers.

As I finished at Repton, the question of my future had to be
decided. My housemaster, Colonel H. Morgan-Owen DSO, was
convinced that I should go into business, and a meeting was
arranged with one of the directors of a famous North of
England biscuit-making firm. I always wondered at the ease
with which an appointment was made with so important a
tycoon until, years later, I read in Bernard Thomas's *Repton
1557–1957*:

In 1929 ... the Headmaster (Geoffrey Fisher) announced that more help was
going to be provided by the School for those boys who were willing to take
industrial posts when they left; the Bursar was to make contacts with big
business firms which wished to employ public school boys, and this as the
start of the Careers Master and the Schools Employment Bureau.

My interview went something like this, the tycoon opening
with some flattering platitudes:

'With your edyercayshun, 'n bein' 'ead of yer 'ouse, 'n a
school prefect, 'n yer football colours, yer'd be a Bake-Arse
manager in nao time.'

'A Bake – er – what, Sir?'

'Arse, Arse, you know, what yer live in, only in our Arses
we bake biscuits, see? Ha, ha!'

Shattered by this horrific prospect I wrote to my father
asking if the family tradition of university could be managed.
To my relief the answer was yes, and I duly entered Trinity
College to read English and French.

Trinity College, Dublin

Being in the centre of a capital city Trinity does not have the
total seclusion of an Oxford or Cambridge college. It is larger,
with great open spaces surrounded by impressive buildings of
different periods, and possesses a unique majesty. Yet on
entering Front Gate one is aware of the bustle of the great city
being left behind, replaced by a quiet, academic serenity.

In 1933 I was allotted rooms in the Graduates' Memorial
Building, my sitting-room overlooking the cobbled Parliament
Square to the right, and immediately in front the spacious
lawns and dignified trees of the Library Square. Between them

stood the commanding Campanile, four-square on its squat legs. My bedroom overlooked Botany Bay, a well-named prison-like square, offering nothing to the eye but a mud-coloured surface and a surround of hideous buildings.

While in these rooms I had a visit from Bill Monk Gibbon, then Ireland's most promising young poet, who came to tea. I remember the spare figure, the neat moustache, the kind eyes, constantly alert as though storing up impressions for future use, and the earnest, musical, enthusiastic voice.

He gave me a copy of *For Daws to Peck At*, and I was struck by the simplicity of some of his poems: 'I know a girl who's like a flower ... ' is a lovely line which misses bathos by a hair's breadth, indicating the mastery of words which can instil magic into a not very original image. I showed him some of my own poems, but cannot recall his comments. However, years later he inscribed a copy of *This Insubstantial Pageant*, 'For Peter Ross, one of whose – many – apocryphal legends is that I ruined a good poet by my savage criticism of his early verses, shown to me when he was a student in Trinity. He can now avenge himself by the acerbity of his pencilled marginalia in this book! Monk Gibbon, Nov. 5th, '68.'

In 1933 what Lord Hailsham called the 'yellow-bellied undergraduates' of the Oxford Union passed their resolution 'that this House refuses to fight for King and Country'. Among the many universities that followed suit was Trinity, Dublin (Ireland was then a member of the Commonwealth). It was a good debate and I spoke forcefully on the subject of pacifism.

A few days later I was sitting at the window of my rooms in the GMB idly admiring the shadowed lawns and some of the young ladies walking across the Front Square, when there came a knock at my door. It was a delegation made up of the most deadly bores and busybodies in college. Their leader asked me to sign the Peace Pledge. Immediately a presentiment made me refuse.

'But you argued so strongly as a pacifist – '

'Maybe, but I don't know how I'll feel in, say, five or six years if there is a war.'

'Isn't that a bit hypocritical?'

'Yes. Goodbye.'

The summer holidays of 1939 were drawing to a close. Only a few days remained before I had to go back to my teaching post in Dorset. County Donegal was at its loveliest. There was autumn gold in the leaves, yet the atmosphere was still that of summer.

A friend, Reginald Osborne, who had recently passed into the Fleet Air Arm, had a boat, a twenty-foot affair of no known pedigree. It was temperamental, but fun to sail, especially among the 'Hundred Islands' of Mulroy Bay. On 1 September I set off by car with my brothers Frank and John to join him in a morning's outing. As we dragged the dinghy down to the water we were hailed by a sailor from the deck of a rusty tramp steamer tied up at the quay. He was very excited.

'It's war,' he shouted, 'it's war!'

'What do you mean?'

'Them Germans has gone into Poland – heard it on the wireless just now!'

The unbelievable, the icy, terrible thing had happened. No one said a word. We rowed out to the yacht and set sail. The breeze was steady but not stiff. For a long time we stayed silent.

'That means war for us,' said Reginald at last. I looked at him. Red hair, blue eyes, pleasant regular features, and a curious crease at the corner of his mouth; you never knew when he would break into laughter. He was young, only eighteen.

'Yes,' I said.

It was easier now that he had broken the spell. The beauty of the country was like an agony in its expression of peace.

We started talking now. As the strengthening wind caught the sails we became forcedly cheerful, as people do when hit by an inescapable calamity. The water rippled by, its surface little excited mirrors, as we rounded the islands and skirted the mainland. We drank a lot of beer, talked a lot of nonsense, and pretended we were enjoying ourselves. The green and yellow fields slid by, the hills stood purple above us. It was all so tranquil.

Then Reginald started singing. He looked far across the water as he held the tiller and sang in a clear tenor voice to himself: 'Little Sir Echo, I'm calling you – Hullo! Hullo! Hullo! ... ' The dreamy notes rose and fell, the nostalgia of the words calling up the shade of the past and saluting the unknown, terrifying future. I have often wondered what Reginald was thinking and feeling with that distant look in his eyes. Less than a year later he was killed when his Swordfish crashed.

Even the tune brings back the sensations of that day, the awareness of a great event coloured almost entirely by the tints of your own private, obscure and unimportant life.

For me, as for everyone, there was the shock realization of a career interrupted, perhaps finished. An honors degree, a silver medal for composition in the University Philosophical Society, editing *T.C.D. – A College Miscellany*, dreams of pursuing a literary career in the long school holidays – the so-important achievements of university life now rendered trivial and ir-relevant.

While the rumours of war were gathering, my father, now retired after a distinguished career in the Indian Public Works Department, joined the Ministry of Home Security. His head-quarters were in Cardiff, where he and my mother rented a house and where I spent holidays until I enlisted in the army.

ONE

Monty

Unknown to me (and presumably to him too), General Bernard
Montgomery and I arrived in the Western Desert within a few
months of each other, I in May and he in August, 1942. From
then on we never lost a battle ...

It is a quality of greatness that it inspires either hero-worship
or loathing: there is no middle path. You were either 'a Monty
man' or you were not. To his many critics I would reply that
his arrival had the effect on the Eighth Army of an electric
shock. At last a clear determined direction was given to those
fine troops who had fought so long, winning so many battles
but never a campaign, and were now back where they started,
on the Alamein line. Monty refused whenever possible to
commit his troops to battle unless he had guns and tanks in
superior numbers, which required the strength of mind to
insist to his superiors that they give him what he wanted. His
clear-cut, boyish orders were easily understood, and we all
knew that with him in command we could not lose.

It is often forgotten that in France in 1940 Monty commanded the 3rd Division, withdrawing them under-equipped and
unsupported from Belgium to Dunkirk, inflicting great casualties upon the enemy. He later wrote:

To exercise high command successfully one has to have an infinite capacity for
taking pains and for careful preparation; and one has also to have an *inner
conviction* which at times will transcend reason.

It was this almost mystical inner conviction which won him so
many enemies, but also unique success.

It is significant that Monty had great admiration for Moses,
to whom the Lord said, 'Certainly I will be with thee.' Furthermore, he concluded an address at the Alamein Memorial:

A great commander once dismissed his troops after a long campaign with these words: 'Choose you this day whom you will serve; as for me and my house, we will serve the Lord' [Joshua 24: 15]. And it was to him that the Lord added, 'Be strong and of a good courage ... for the Lord thy God is with thee.'

Monty appears to have consciously identified with these Old Testament leaders, which would have been appreciated by his father, Bishop of Tasmania, whom he worshipped.

Preparation

Looking back now I can string together the sequence of events that led to my presence at Alamein. In 1941 I was commissioned into a famous cavalry regiment, recently equipped with tanks, among whose battle honours Balaclava ranked high and whose forbears had suffered severe casualties in the Charge of the Light Brigade. Their obsession with the past was equalled only by their obsession with horses, two aspects of an approach to modern warfare which filled me with apprehension.

On my way to join the regiment I met another officer, called Tony, a new boy like myself. We were posted to the same squadron. His father was a brigadier in the regular army, and he himself a university lecturer in English. We had much in common and enjoyed our conversation, which we continued during dinner that evening in the mess, a small dark room in a requisitioned farmhouse in Buckinghamshire.

After dinner the Second-in-Command came over to us.

'The Squadron Leader's compliments, gentlemen. He reminds you that officers may not initiate conversations in the mess until they have been members for three months.'

As he spoke the Squadron Leader was seated in an armchair not three yards from us, immersed in the only book I ever saw in that mess, Hadley Chase's *No Orchids for Miss Blandish*. Such formality was impressive, but it cast a chill over Tony and myself, neither of us being noted for taciturnity.

Next day I was allotted to a troop, which was very different from having a troop allotted to me. Technically I was second-in-command. In fact I was supernumerary. Sidney, the Troop Officer, was a highly efficient and mechanically minded young man who had his wits about him. He was a rarity in the regiment, his first interest being tanks and his last horses, and consequently rather an outcast. The Troop Sergeant, called

'Lofty' on account of his lack of stature, had been decorated for gallantry in France in 1940 and regarded me as an ingenuous and idle greenhorn who "adn't never 'eard a shot fired in anger'. The men had one main word in their monotonous vocabulary, 'browned-off', qualified, of course, by the Universal Epithet.

Such was my uninspiring situation when we set off, one week after my arrival, on the famous 'Exercise Bumper'. The greatest manoeuvre ever carried out in Britain, it involved all services, civilian as well as military. Our brigade represented the spearhead of a Nazi invasion force which, after a successful landing in East Anglia, was deemed to be driving south-westwards towards Oxford. We did very well to begin with, and caused quite a stir as we passed through villages and towns, undeterred even when the *Luftwaffe* dropped a real incendiary bomb near us one night as we leaguered in a field. Soon, however, it became apparent that we were not making the progress we should. Finally our advance came to a halt, the umpires deciding that we had lost nearly all our tanks. Information became scarce; we had no idea whether we had 'won' or 'lost': certainly we had not breached our objective, the Oxford–Reading line. Years afterwards I learned that the officer commanding our opponents was a certain General Montgomery.

My own part in this exercise was undistinguished. In one town where we halted at night I jumped out of my tank with such eagerness that I forgot to remove my earphones. As the flex jerked them off, forcing my head back almost to the point of dislocation, I was aware of a bright flash from inside the tank, not, as I thought, a direct hit from an incendiary bomb, but a short circuit caused by the rapid disconnection. As I lay bruised and humiliated in the gutter, surrounded by a group of grinning townsmen, our Squadron Leader strode over and relieved me of my command.

I was now given the job of Liaison Officer, it being supposed, I think, that I would then be as harmless as possible. One night we leaguered in the vast estate of the Duke of Bedford at Woburn. I was sent on a mission some miles away and during my return the heavens opened with a downpour of monsoon-like intensity. Riding a powerful and extremely heavy motorbike at night in the black-out, with no lights, was bad enough; but now, with visibility limited to a few yards,

blinded by the rain, which began to pour down my neck and
seep through my thick overcoat, and chilled already by the
autumnal night, I was in a state of utter misery and fatigue.

As the last dregs of energy were draining out of me I saw a
small, low building at the side of the laneway. Inspecting it
with my torch, the use of which was a reckless and desperate
act, I recognized it as a well-built stone henhouse, with a slated
roof. I lifted the little doorway and crept in on all fours. The
floor was concrete but it was dry, and I was exhausted. The
thunderous rain on the roof made it impossible to know if I
had company, since my torch suddenly ceased to work. The
arrival of a warm, wet 'bomb' in my left ear made it clear that I
was not alone. The continuous bombardment which this
heralded was preferable to the ferocious downpour.

When dawn came I saw that at least a dozen hens were
perched above me. As I crawled out I felt grateful to them.
They hadn't really resented my intrusion, yet didn't feel it
necessary to make any concessions on my behalf.

Squadron HQ was in a small clearing in a wood. My arrival
was marked by expressions of distaste on the faces of the
senior officers, and suppressed mirth on those of the less
elevated. I could understand the Squadron Leader's attitude to
my appearance, and the odour which accompanied it: after all,
this was a crack regiment where smartness held high priority.
Unfortunately the incident reinforced his disapproval of me,
from then on expressed more and more cuttingly, which further undermined my confidence, already frail where military
matters were concerned.

Things came to a head the following spring. We were camped
near Marlborough and I was put in charge of squadron stores.
Together with the Quartermaster I had the hut scrubbed and
the windows cleaned, and then set about rearranging the
equipment and making a new inventory. We worked with
enthusiasm and the result looked superb. I reported to the
Squadron Leader, confident that at last I had done something
deserving his praise. He came to inspect our work, turned on
his heel and said, 'It's absolutely filthy – I want it perfect by
tonight!'

With a feeling of utter dejection and hopelessness I set off
across the sunlit camp towards the mess for lunch. The Adjutant

emerged from his office and fell in beside me.

'Two officers wanted from the brigade for the Middle East,' he said. 'Know of anyone who might be interested?'

'Yes I do!' I replied, '*I* am interested – very!'

'Right,' he said, 'I'll go back to the orderly room and put your name forward.'

Five minutes later he appeared in the mess.

'You're booked. You go on embarkation leave tomorrow, and report to Aldershot in ten days' time.'

Embarkation Leave

Standing beside my mother on the platform at Cardiff at the end of my embarkation leave, I could feel the anxiety and sorrow that racked her. She had been very ill, and was therefore doubly sensitive to what might be in store for her three sons. I remember talking quickly to avoid any emotional scene, wishing she would say goodbye now before one of us broke down, but she wanted to savour every moment. At last the quick kiss, jumping into the empty carriage, taking a last glimpse at the forlorn little figure on the platform. After a final, formal wave, I sat back, realizing how alone I was, caught up in a sequence of events into which I had willingly entered, but over which I now had no control.

The weather was warm and sunny, the countryside rushing by was fresh in the spring. I stared out, trying to memorize it, knowing I might never see it again. Feeling somewhat in the mould of Rupert Brooke I started a poem: 'Goodbye is a slow throbbing in the heart.'

My assignment was to the Middle East, a vast area including Syria, Palestine, Egypt. Each held promise of adventure, though the Western Desert was the only scene of any action. The one time I had set foot in Egypt was for a day in 1936, on my way to spend a few months with my father in India. It was the conventional stop-off of the period – a visit to Simon Artz to buy a topee, and a bathe in the Med.

Now I had said goodbye to my mother, my father and my brothers. I realized that war must be worse for those waiting for news, which is often dilatory and sometimes wrong, than for those engaged in battle, whose thoughts can be only of the matter in hand.

Interim

People sometimes talk of their lives having a pattern. Perhaps
near the end one might look back and see some unbroken
strand conspicuous in the warp and woof, and say, There! that
was my destiny – from poverty to riches, or was it from riches
to poverty? For few of us, however, is this true. For certain
periods there might be a continuity, such as one's schooldays,
or the years spent in a particular job, and afterwards these
might seem to have produced a pattern; but it is unlikely that
anyone is aware of it at the time, in most cases a patchwork
being more evident than a pattern.

My few days at Aldershot before embarkation stand out like
a bridge over a stream, connecting my months of military
training with the years of active service which followed, yet
part of neither.

One night a dance was given by the ATS. It was a huge
success. The senior officers were able to show off their blues,
and we subalterns to cut a pretty figure at the bar and on the
floor. The girls, officers and privates, were outnumbered five to
one, so that even the Plainest Jane could be sure of having
every dance or, at worst, sitting it out with a glass of beer and a
Real Live Officer.

I was with a group of fellow draft officers propping up the
bar when the Adjutant, sweat pouring from his rather birdy
face, passed close to us as he jitterbugged the pretty Mess
Corporal round the floor.

'Who was that you winked at?' I heard him ask. He seemed
piqued.

'Only one of the draft officers.'

He eyed us with distaste and clutched her closer to him.

The music ceased, to an enthusiastic burst of clapping. The
band firmly announced that it had played the last encore for
that dance by rattling a staccato on the drums. The couple
walked towards the bar.

'What'll you drink?' asked the Adjutant, trying to steer his
partner past us.

'I'll have a – '

'Hullo, Hilda!' I said quickly, catching her by the arm, 'I've
got a drink for you here – and the next dance is mine!'

The Adjutant glared at me. 'Bloody war-time officers,' he

muttered thickly, 'no reshpect, don' know how to behave ... 'He drifted unsteadily away.

Hilda mopped her brow. 'Whew, what an effort!'

'What! Don't you like him? I'd have thought he was just your type!'

'Oo? 'Im? Old Birdseed? You 'ave got a cheek!'

The vivacity in her voice made me look closely at her. Dark, bright-eyed, slim, trim in her uniform. I remember thinking, rather smugly, that the war had brought something into this little Cockney's life that she would never have found in peace-time.

'Have another,' someone said.

'Yes please, may I have a short?'

'My God, that was quick work. What, that pint gone already?'

'Yes, I'm celebrating today. It's my birthday. Twenty-first,' she added.

'I don't believe it. Let's see your AB 64 Part One!'

'All right, 'ere you are, disbelievin' Joo.'

'Let's see – hm – yes, quite right. Very interesting – married, too. Well, well – '

'Come orf it!' She poked him in the ribs, seized her book, and giggled.

'Married?' I cried, 'and doesn't wear a wedding-ring! Naughty, naughty, encouraging the Adjutant like that!'

When the band struck up again I led her onto the floor. It was a waltz, a dainty, hesitant thing that appealed to me with its quiet rhythm and sentimental words.

'You're very quiet!'

'Hm? Oh yes, sorry.'

I had been miles away, back in Donegal. The summer of 1938 was fine and was spent playing tennis with friends, climbing the heathered hills, ambling round the little Otway golf-links on the shore of Lough Swilly.

I was thinking of one of those exquisite days that sometimes take you by surprise in Donegal; the light with a brittle quality; the half-door of a cottage on a distant mountain. The stillness was never total because all the time you could hear the faint shock of the waves as they slid among the pebbles of the cove between the Martello Tower and the little headland. The water was deceptively inviting. We always carried our bathing-togs when playing golf and, by mutual consent, my father and I plunged in from the fourth fairway, which bordered the curving beach. Two sharp yelps escaped us and we rushed back to dry and get some warmth in us by playing on.

'You're very quiet!'

It was no good luxuriating in reminiscence now. And it was unpardonable to desert Hilda for even a minute's reverie, Hilda, whose warm body and lovely skin were beginning to grip my attention. I enjoyed the absurdity of the situation, dancing with this attractive, happy girl whom I would never meet again after tonight, and whom I would never have met at all if it hadn't been for the war; the war to save a democracy that could really be a social democracy only during a war.

'Who are you dancing with next?' I asked.

'A Polish officer.'

'Oh, Hilda! Very dangerous. Now you must be careful! A Polish officer! Tch! Tch! I hope you'll be safe.'

'He's ever so attractive!'

'Now you're making me jealous.'

'Go on!'

At this point a beer-sodden Major barged in upon us, spluttering 'Excuse me!' with a lecherous leer at Hilda and a triumphal glare at me.

Damn, I thought. Always the way at these army hops. Excuse-me dances ... What an invention, and purely for the benefit of unattractive over-sexed men who couldn't otherwise find a partner. I stalked off towards the bar, chewing my disgruntlement.

There I found the Adjutant, consoling himself with Scotch. He smirked at me.

'Pipped? Too bad. Have a drink. Nice little piece that Corporal, eh?'

'I'll say.'

'Very hot, very hot. But you want to be careful, ol' boy, ver' careful. Womensh all right in their place, y'know, which is bed, not the army, eh? Ha ha!'

I tried not to cringe. 'Have another,' I said.

'Another? Haven't had one yet. But I've got my eye on that Corporal. She's nice. Extra speshul – er – nice.' He swayed slightly.

'Women,' he said ruminatively, 'all womensh ni ... er ... what I said. All all all right in the black-out. What'sh time?'

'Ten-fifteen.'

'Too bad – not dark enough yet. Better have another drink.'

We did. We had several.

After a bit I went to find the Corporal, but the next dance was a Paul Jones, so I gave up and returned to the bar. The Adjutant had gone.

It was a good hour before I danced with her again. The heat was overwhelming by now. We had hardly started when Hilda said she wanted to sit it out. We found a place near the door.

'Ooh! I feel sick,' she sighed.

'My God!' I looked at her. 'What have you been drinking?'

'Gin.'

'Gin! Who gave you that?'

'And rum.'

'Where the hell did you get it?'

'From Petrov – Petrov – whatsishname.'

'That Pole! You silly little fool – mixing them like that!'

'I want to be sick.'

'All right, come on.' I wheeled her past the red-capped MP at the door, who, I thought, gave me a dirty wink as we stepped into the black-out.

'Now,' I said, 'we'll walk. We'll walk flat out up and down this parade-ground until you feel better – or until you're sick.'

We started off, neither of us saying a word. The Corporal was steering an erratic course. I put my arm round her waist to steady her.

'Thanks.' She stopped, leaned up, and kissed me. I hoped she wasn't going to puke.

At that moment a light shone upon us.

'Halt! Who goes there!'

'Friend,' I answered, thanking God I was leaving the next day.

'Advance one, and be reckernized!'

'You go first,' I whispered. 'Can you make it?' She could, just.

'Advance two!'

I went forward, giving my rank and name, explaining that we would be back that way shortly.

'Pass, friend.'

We walked on into the black-out.

'Feeling better?' I took her arm.

'Yes.'

'Tell me, are you really married?'

'No.' I thought she was laughing.

'Engaged?' I could feel her trembling, and knew it wasn't laughter.

'Hey!' I exclaimed, 'you mustn't cry!'

'I *was* engaged,' she said. 'Philip – he was in – in Singapore. Nothing's been heard of him.'

She was crying now like a child, hopelessly, without any effort at control. I didn't know what to say. My earlier thought that the war had brought something to this girl that peace could never bring had, in an ironic way, been right.

I took her by the shoulders and shook her gently, knowing that I had no balm to ease her pain.

'Come on, it may be all right in the end. Lots of those chaps got away. Don't be afraid.'

'I am afraid.'

'Steady,' I urged, 'Philip wouldn't want you to cry.'

'I know.' Pressing a wet handkerchief to her eyes, she smiled as though trying to force back the tears.

'Shall we go back to the dance?' I suggested.

'Yes.'

'Well, first you'd better try to mop your face up. Here's a dry handkerchief.'

As we went in we met the Adjutant.

'So that'sh where you've been!' He lurched drunkenly towards me. 'Been looking for you everywhere. Canoodlin' in the black-out, eh?'

'Bloody fool!' I thought, and laughed to appease him.

Then I swung Hilda out onto the dance-floor.

Next day we were informed that our departure date had been postponed and leave of absence granted for two days – too short for us to go home and too long for us to stay put. Four of us decided to spend this bonus time in London. Neville and I booked into the Strand Palace, John and Dick into the Regent Palace, and we arranged to meet after dinner at a pub in Leicester Square.

It was a fine night, too fine for air raids, so we went confident-
ly out in search of fun, arrogant in our cavalry-cut uniforms,
our regimental-coloured side-caps jauntily perched on our
heads. John and Dick were already gracing the bar when we
arrived.

'Good news,' John greeted us. 'Party of WAAFs meeting us
after closing-time at the Regent Pal. Come and help us enter-
tain them.'

We chatted and drank until nearly closing-time and then
walked out into the darkened street. John and Dick were a few
steps ahead of me. I realized that Neville was missing, assumed
he'd forgotten something and walked on. There was a tap on
my shoulder and Neville, breathless, said, 'There's a girl in the
pub wants to talk to you.'

'What about?'

'How the hell should I know?'

Annoyed, I turned back. I had seen four or five women in
civilian dress on a bench behind us, but as they were absorbed
in their own talk had taken no further notice. When I arrived
the barman was calling out 'Time, please!' The girls arose and
one of them came towards me.

'Could I talk to you, please?'

'I suppose so. What about?'

'Can we walk a bit?'

I agreed resignedly and hoped she'd be quick, as I was
looking forward to joining the party in the Regent Palace. I
thought perhaps she needed money.

She was good-looking in a flabby way, big-boned, cheaply
dressed, yet dignified and tidy. She slipped her hand through
my arm and began. Her husband, she explained, was a
sergeant. He was posted as an instructor at a training regiment
in the north of England, and had been there for six months. She
had discovered that he was carrying on with girls up there. At
first she had been unhappy, now she wanted revenge.

'What do you expect me to do?' I asked. 'Officers have no
jurisdiction over people in other units. Why don't you write to
his CO?'

She ignored my question. 'There *is* something I'd like you to
do,' she said in a hushed voice.

'What? Shoot him?' I laughed.

'No. I'd like you to go to bed with me tonight. If he does it, why shouldn't I?'

Her words made me stop. They were so unexpected, like something in a mad film. As I looked at her in the darkness I felt a strange answering sensation coursing through my body. This might be my last leave ever and fortune was offering me now a comfort and excitement that I might have wished for but never found. All honourable considerations were suddenly numbed.

'All right,' I said. 'Where do you live?'

'Hammersmith.'

'Oh my God – that's miles! No, I couldn't go out there.' I didn't add that I had an urgent appointment at the Regent Palace which I didn't want to miss. She seemed to crumble, so I said hastily, 'All right, all right, we'll go to my hotel.'

We sat in the lounge.

'I don't know how strict they are in this hotel. My room's on the first floor. Here's the key, the number's on it. Walk up as if you owned the place and I'll follow you in a minute or two.'

I watched her going up that vast staircase. She moved well, but I felt no sexual attraction.

Soon I went up. I knocked, and she let me in. She had taken off her blouse but not her bra, and was still wearing her black skirt and shoes. As I walked towards her I felt it might not be so unexciting to undress her.

'Would you turn out the light?' she said shyly. I did so. As I undressed I heard her slide into the bed. Her body was warm and soft, her breasts unfirm and drooping. A mother, I guessed. We enjoyed each other briefly and perfunctorily. Afterwards we lay relaxed, not speaking. In a little while, as if by mutual agreement, we got up and dressed.

Outside the hotel I hailed a taxi. I decided I should see her home. On the way she said, 'That'll teach him!'

'What! You're not going to tell him?'

'Of course – what's the point if I don't?'

Coming back in the taxi I pondered this strange affair. In a way I was flattered. She had chosen me out of all the officers present – though I had to admit she was not carried away just by my charm.

At the Regent Palace I found John, Dick and Neville sitting

in an alcove with four WAAFs. Everyone was tight, so every-one was happy. Myrtle – what a name! – moved up as I approached and I sat beside her. Being sober I had to bury my critical sense and I smiled at Myrtle. She was almost lovely. Fair, not quite blonde, high cheek-bones, a generous mouth which widened into warm smiles revealing even but rather large teeth. She seemed more sober than the others.

A short, firm pressure made me realize that her hand was in mine. This surprised me, and I looked deeply into those big, inviting eyes.

'Shall we go upstairs?' I heard myself asking.

She nodded. 'Yes, but we must go now before my room-mate comes up.'

The lift was empty when we entered. Before I could press the button a huge man in a grey suit hurled himself in. He looked strong and athletic, the sort of Tarzan music-halls employ as a bouncer. From the moment he came in he stared at us. There was no particular expression on his face but one sensed disapproval. An Air Force Padre, perhaps, in civvies? He had an Air Force aura about him – debonair, fearless, impulsive. Or a vigilante appointed by the hotel authorities (of all people!) to preserve morality among their patrons? You never knew. I would have felt no surprise if he had pulled a religious tract from his pocket and handed it to me with a menacing look – refuse that if you dare! Nor if he had followed us to the room, stood in front of the door and silently refused us entry. As it happened he did neither. We got out at the third floor and he continued up.

Myrtle took off her jacket and lay down on one of the beds. The irony of my situation made me smile – two attractive girls inviting me to bed within a few hours of each other, and behind and before me so many lonely lengthy nights. Now I began to regret the earlier adventure because Myrtle was young and lovely and I hoped that my vengeful friend had not drained all my powers.

I undid Myrtle's tie and unbuttoned her shirt. She didn't help, neither did she impede. Her shape was slender and finely proportioned. I bent to kiss her breasts. She held my head close to her and whispered, 'Would you mind if we didn't tonight? I might go to sleep in the middle!'

It was with relief that I acceded. In fact I was tired too, and my vanity was spared the humiliation of my seeming impotent.

'Did old sour-face in the lift put you off?'

'Not really,' she giggled sleepily, 'but he didn't help!'

I kissed her and laid her head upon the pillow. She was fast asleep.

TWO

Voyage to Egypt

The *Queen Mary*, painted grey as the surrounding mist, moved slowly down the Clyde. There was a tense speculative silence among her passengers, whose future seemed symbolized by that envelope of mist, obscure, frightening, yet offering some hidden promise of adventure.

The name *Queen Mary* spelt luxury and ease in her peace-time role. Now, at war, she packed 16,000 passengers into a space intended for half that number. These were sailors, soldiers, airmen, an ATS unit, and nursing sisters; reinforcements for the Eighth Army in Egypt.

At first we were accompanied by a destroyer but, as the great liner gathered speed, this fell behind. No ship could store enough fuel to keep up with her for more than thirty-six hours, so she travelled long distances in majestic solitude, relying on her pace to evade hostile submarines and warships.

The 700 draft officers, 60 nursing sisters and the ATS unit used the first-class lounge. A small corner, known as the Virgins' Retreat, was cordoned off for those ladies who might want some temporary peace from suitors who were all the more ardent because of the boredom induced by inactivity. Staterooms intended for two passengers were now modified to hold eighteen officers. Uncomfortable as this was, it was nothing to the conditions endured by the other ranks. So tightly were they packed, and so inadequate their feeding arrangements, that those at the back of the queue had to wait three hours for their meals. A man, therefore, who had waited from 6 a.m. till 9 a.m. for his breakfast would have to start queuing again at 10 a.m. for his lunch. Owing to their number, and to the strict black-out regulations, it was impossible for a third of the men at any one time to find somewhere to read or write letters or play cards. No one seemed to take much interest in them because, with a few exceptions, the drafts were travelling without officers, and few of the officers themselves had men attached to them.

The boredom, the lack of space, the discomforts caused by faulty organization, the vile stuffiness and stenches inevitable on board an overcrowded liner designed for transatlantic temperatures and not the heat of equatorial zones; these, and the apprehension of what could happen during the voyage or at its end, accentuated the irritation and irony of living like pigs among the trappings of luxury.

We anchored for a few days off Freetown. The buildings shimmered whitely in the heat haze while we looked ashore with curiosity. Little black boys in bum-boats chattered and showed off, dived for pennies, grinned and exchanged obscenities with the troops. The heat was of that damp, throbbing quality which denies all pleasurable pastime. We sweated and longed for the moment when we would weigh anchor and the movement of the ship would cause a breeze. Evening brought a delicious coolness, but this never penetrated below decks.

Soon we were on our way again. Next stop Capetown, and a few hours ashore! Morale rose. We could hear singing from the men's quarters, and in the officers' lounge the mood was more for dancing and chatting than reading or playing chess or cards. Not for long, however. Someone committed what was officially described as A Breach of Discipline. Unofficially it was whispered that a French letter had been found in the scuppers during Captain's Rounds. Immediate action was taken: all men and women, officers and other ranks, had to be below decks between the hours of 6 p.m. and 6 a.m. It was never explained what we were being punished for: whether because the decks had been littered with refuse, which is quite rightly considered a dreadful crime in the Royal Navy, under whose discipline we were now living; or because of the moral implications of the type of refuse involved, of which delicacy on the part of the senior officers prevented mention, since we were a mixed company.

Feeling among all ranks was intense. The mood became one of grim, resentful bad temper. In the officers' lounge boredom led to quarrelling, aggravated by drink. It must have been worse in the men's quarters. We didn't know; we were not allowed to go there, authority apparently imagining that discipline among the drafts could safely be left to the NCOs.

However, we remembered stories of the reception given by the kindly folk of South Africa to the British troops off the convoys. Anticipation of this treat offset some of the gloom as we sailed from Freetown, accompanied by a Catalina flying boat, and sped along the south-west coast of Africa.

As we neared Capetown the weather broke, and we were followed by a heavy swell. We entered the bay in the evening, weaving our way slowly through a large convoy of troopships already anchored there. The *Queen Mary* towered above the ships as we passed close enough for the exchange of courtesies usual between British troops.

'Get up off your knees!' yelled one wag from our foredeck as we passed a small liner.

'Ye'll be on yer own when you've been ashore for a few hours!' was the promising rejoinder from a red-headed Scotsman.

The massive ship was rolling when she found her anchorage and the lighters came alongside with difficulty. There were hoots of encouraging derision as OC Troops, his face now as red as his tabs, was helped none too gently by some ratings into a pinnace. Obviously he was going ashore at considerable personal risk to make arrangements for our reception and accommodation. The men gave him a cheer.

When night fell we watched with wonder the unblacked-out beauty of the city as it put on its sparkling finery, inviting us to join the jubilations and the feast. Sequins glinting through the darkness, it lay like a huge Spanish shawl negligently thrown down the side of Table Mountain. Our anticipation was whetted by the boatloads of singing troops from the convoy as they passed with practised nonchalance and disappeared towards the shore. We counted our money and speculated on the length of our stay.

Next day the ship was still rolling. No orders were posted about shore leave. And so it was the next day, and the next. Still, we were prepared to be patient, for this was really worth waiting for. But the rolling of the great ship did not diminish and, until it did, going ashore was impossible.

Then, suddenly, without warning, we put to sea, leaving behind us the convoy and our unfulfilled hopes.

Durban! Of course, that was it! Capetown was overcrowded with troops, and so we would be put ashore at Durban, which had the reputation of being even more hospitable than Capetown.

That night we received three pieces of dramatic news. First a notice was posted by OC Troops that since the swell at Capetown had made refuelling difficult, all ranks must use the utmost economy with water, as we would not be putting ashore again. Then the BBC news announced that a Japanese submarine was operating in the Mozambique Channel and had sunk several ships; and, as a final shaft at our morale, that the Eighth Army was retreating towards Egypt.

We moved that night into the dark waters washing the Cape of Good Hope, which seemed ill-named in these circumstances. There was in fact an atmosphere of hopelessness and helplessness on board, concocted of disappointment, boredom and suspense. Our position as pawns in the game was now acutely clear to us. The very purpose of our journey would be rendered futile if the Eighth Army failed to hold the Germans. What would happen then? Ignominious return to the UK? Or diversion to India? Discussion was interminable and fruitless, as all discussions must be when you have no control over the situation and no facts to go on, only doubts and fears about your own future.

Such moods are always aggravated when there is no real work to be done. The main task of the draft officers, censoring letters, took up only an hour or so in the morning. Reading these letters, which induced an unpleasant feeling of trespassing on private ground, opened my eyes to two things, one rewarding, the other not.

The first was the delightful simplicity of some men's minds: 'Dear Queenie and Mary, you'll never guess what ship I'm on, and of course I can't tell you ... ' The second was the cruelty sometimes instigated by agony. When I had to plough through a letter like this I never read the signature in case I might meet the man later on: 'Bill says yore going out with Harry and going to his house which is easy for you me being away, just remember yore my wife and I'll tell you what I'll do when I get back, I'll put you on the kitchen table and take off yore pants and beat you till you cant take no more ... '

When one had ground one's way through a few hundred or so of these illuminating documents, cut out a few offending (in the military sense) passages with a pair of scissors, licked the envelopes, initialled them and delivered them to the Security Officer, one gravitated to the bar.

One morning, half an hour or so before lunch, I found there a senior naval officer and fell into conversation with him.

'Bloody ship, this,' he said as he lowered his sixth pink gin, 'no use on a run like this. Do you know that a man is buried at sea every third night? Shoot 'em out at the stern. Can't take it. Too hot. Or too much liquor.' He glanced at his watch. 'Time we went down to lunch. Keep a place for me, old boy, I'll join you in a few minutes.'

I found an empty table set for four, and sat down. Soon I was joined by two naval officers.

'Saw you drinking with X,' one of them said. 'He's a hard case, quite indestructible. How many pink gins did he have with you? Six? Well, he'd had six with me before that! But he'll come down here, eat his lunch, chat away, and you wouldn't know he'd touched a drop!'

But he didn't come down, and he wasn't in the bar that evening, nor at the pre-lunch session next day. So I enquired at the office.

'Commander X? Commander X was buried overboard last night.'

The novelty and excitement of travelling on this great ship had long worn off. The overcrowding and the heat made most activities unpleasant and some impossible. A surly spirit of boredom, exacerbated by the disappointment at Capetown, now pervaded the officers' lounge. Tempers were lost at cards; people drank in order to escape the boredom, and then quarrelled. There seemed nothing new to talk about; the books had all been read; and the music piped through the amplifiers, even though it included the famous Warsaw Concerto, was becoming repetitive and annoying. We heard stories of discontent and fighting among the other ranks, but this caused only a brief ripple in our apathy.

Then one day we were summoned by the officer commanding

our deck. He was a wing commander with aquiline features
and a tanned complexion who had been awarded the MC in
the First World War and the DSO and DFC in the Second. As
soon as we were gathered in his cabin he began to speak,
quietly and with authority.

'If we're not very careful there's going to be a mutiny on
board this ship. I needn't tell you how serious that would be.
I've seen it happen before, and I know the signs. There is no
singing or whistling; the men huddle together in little groups,
talking in undertones, and are silent when an officer passes;
they don't salute unless it's absolutely forced upon them; they
stand about and pretend they don't see you coming, so that
you have to push your way past; and they mock collectively at
officers from a safe distance.'

He paused for a moment and looked at each one of us in
turn, as if trying to assess the effect of his words.

'Now, I want you all to go out on deck and walk round a bit.
Come back here in twenty minutes and tell me if you think
what I say is true.'

We dispersed and followed the Wing Commander's instructions. It was as he said, and now we realized that what had
previously seemed nothing more than a vague discontent was
something far more dangerous. An air of hostility was
sweeping through the ship, a growling, fearsome undertow of
malevolent energy. As he walked the deck an officer felt he
was being watched by a hundred pairs of eyes, yet it was
impossible to meet one of them with his own. He moved in a
vacuum of silence: a grumble of conversation ahead of him and
behind him, but silence where he walked. Men sprawled
insolently on the deck, legs stretched deliberately, so that he
had to pick his way awkwardly among them. His approach
was ignored pointedly, and an order to make way was met
with feigned stupidity, the crowd of onlookers maintaining the
barrage of silence.

We returned to the Wing Commander, alarmed and appre-
hensive, and reported our findings.

'You'll agree we've got to act, and act now. The men have
genuine grievances which we cannot put right – but at least we
can do something to avert trouble. They're bored; we're going
to keep them amused. They don't sing; we'll make 'em sing.

They don't talk; we'll give 'em something to talk about. They don't show respect; we're going to show them where their respect is due. I've seen OC Troops. He approves of my plan, which is this: every morning there will be PT classes, twenty minutes for each man. That will take some organizing, but it will be done. Every day from 2 p.m. till 10 p.m. there will be concerts and singsongs, so every man will be able to look forward to at least one show lasting half an hour each day. You people have got to organize that. Every week there will be two boxing tournaments. And if any of you have any more ideas, let's have 'em.'

Ordinarily one would have left with a sense of depression, feeling that one had been told to do the impossible. How could raw young officers with no administrative experience cope with such a situation? And how did he expect us to provide entertainment good enough to satisfy the troops – especially in their present mood? But his quiet authority, and his urgency, left us clear that there was no room for failure.

We started our planning at once round a table in the lounge. It was proposed that I should take on the Physical Training as I had recently attended a course in that eccentric activity at Aldershot. The fact that I had missed three-quarters of it through illness impressed no one, and I was unanimously elected. One of our number turned out to be a professional comedian in civilian life, which may have accounted for his perpetually pessimistic air. Another had experience of amateur dramatics and had written some one-act plays. This was promising. Our next step was to recruit some talent from among the men.

In no time we had collected a useful little band, consisting of an accordionist, a man with a cornet, and another with a violin. Word got round that we needed helpers, and many who could sing or recite came forward. This was our first victory, getting the men on our side.

For the evening performances we found a covered-in portion of the deck where we were allowed a minute blue light. The band would play some favourite tune such as 'There'll be blue-birds over the white cliffs of Dover' and soon there would be a great gathering of men sitting squeezed together, nostalgia banishing discontent for a while as they sang and whistled. Our compère was an officer who had been a professional actor before the war. We called him 'Boots' because, for reasons known only to himself, he always wore his ammunition boots, even with service dress. Between songs he told stories, vintage and generally clean, with a genius of manner that made him the greatest favourite at these concerts. He used to ask the men what song they wanted next. One night a wag at the back shouted 'Boots!' There was a roar of laughter.

'All right,' retorted Boots, 'but I won't be the only one sloggin' over Africa soon!'

Another roar of laughter, and immediately that three-man band of ours, never defeated, struck up with Kipling's marching song:

> We're foot-slog-slog-slog-sloggin' over Africa –
> Foot-foot-foot-foot-sloggin' over Africa –
> (Boots-boots-boots-boots-movin'-up an' down again!)
> There's no discharge in the war!

The average nightly attendance of 2000 men proved the urgency of filling the dangerous vacuum caused by boredom.

Occasionally we put on a play for the officers. It was agreed that each of us would take part at one time or another, even if only as prompter. Once, when carrying out this important role for a play I had written myself, I was astonished to hear some unscripted dialogue.

'What were you in Civvy Street?'

'A feather plucker.'

'A clever *what*?'

Next day I found myself at attention in front of OC Troops. He explained that the lady standing beside his desk, the colonel commanding the ATS draft, had complained that one of her girls had objected to some – er – rather – er – tasteless lines in the previous night's performance.

'Downright indecent, Sir!' barked the lady, who was trimly uniformed, tie, jacket and all, despite the intense heat. If she'd had a moustache it would have bristled. I was imagining what this would look like when I realized that she was inspecting me with the expression of distaste people adopt when the cat has disgraced itself on the carpet.

OC Troops seemed to expect me to say something. I was seething with injustice, given that the offending lines had surprised me as much as the ladies, so I decided to play dumb.

Feeling a period of outraged silence would strengthen my position, I waited a while and then said in a pained tone, 'I was most careful, Sir, to see that there was nothing offensive in the play. Perhaps the Colonel would tell us exactly what *were* the words complained of?'

' – mm – yes – mm – I think that's – er – fair, eh, Colonel?'

He looked at her, one tufty eyebrow raised, and waited.

She ruled her lips into a straight line and glared at me. Her mouth opened slightly and she took a deep breath. The tips of her top teeth pressed down on her lower lip, and for one glorious moment I thought she was going to say 'feather plucker'. OC Troops looked at her as if he expected her to say something else and a look of alarmed horror tortured his face as he glanced hastily at me and then more hastily looked down at the papers on his desk.

The ATS Colonel expelled her breath in one rush.

'F-f-for crying out loud!' she exploded. 'Men!'

As the door crashed behind her OC Troops placed his hands on the desk in a conclusive manner. But he looked bemused.

'Feather plucker,' he muttered, frowning, 'feather plucker? I don't get it. Feather ... what's wrong with that? Women! And as for you, GET OUT!'

My task as officer-in-charge of PT classes was really a matter of working out a timetable and supervising its implementation. There were several qualified instructors aboard from the army school of PT, who had of course been enlisted in our scheme. My chief assistant was the senior among them, a warrant officer with a blunt turn of phrase. Very early one morning on a tour of inspection we stopped to watch a class being taken by an extremely junior second lieutenant. The men were seated on the deck doing arm exercises.

Thinking of the problems I had overcome so cunningly when making out the timetable, I remarked smugly, 'Everything under control!'

'Bloody fool!' was the shattering reply.

'Who! What do you mean?' I stuttered, thinking I was under a mutinous personal attack.

'Look at 'em,' he went on, ignoring my incoherence, 'sitting on their arses on the wet deck what's just been washed down! Like a lot of fuckin' ducks on a pond. Sure way to give 'em piles!'

For the remainder of the voyage we worked as we had never worked before, giving PT classes in the morning, arranging, rehearsing and putting on concerts for the rest of the day. We forgot the war and the grimly doubtful purpose of our journey, we forgot everything except our tiredness.

But the Wing Commander's plan worked. Had he lacked the foresight and ability to call on his experience, as apparently did every other officer on board, the results would have been incalculable. At best, a few men and officers would have been killed; at worst, the Eighth Army would have lost the equivalent of a division of reinforcements at the time when they were most needed. There was no mention in despatches for the Wing Commander, not that it would have crossed his mind that he had done anything worthy of note.

My final memory of the *Queen Mary* concerns a steward, one of the regulars, used to fat tips from opulent peace-time passengers. It had been published in orders that a universal rate of tipping would be adopted by officers, no tip to exceed £1-0-0. In fact, our steward's only activity throughout the voyage had been complaining that the class of passenger now carried by the *Queen Mary* was not what he was used to.

On the last day the Major commanding our draft called this steward and handed him a pound note.

'Wot's this, Sir?' the man demanded with eyebrows raised.

'Well, if you don't want it, give it back!' The Major stretched out his hand, laughing.

'We usually gets a fiver from officers on this run.'

'Do you? Well, you're only getting a quid this time.'

"Ave a 'eart, Sir,' the man whined. 'You're going to the desert – it's not as if you need the money – you'll likely get killed in the fighting, and I've got a wife and kiddies to look after ... '

THREE

Base Depot

The base depot of the Royal Armoured Corps was at Abassia, a suburb of Cairo. Officers and men were dumped there to acclimatize, then claimed as reinforcements for one of the units in the desert. Life seemed to consist of listening to the experienced war-horses refighting their desert battles in the mess, and an interminable series of technical courses.

The one I enjoyed most was navigation. We were taught the use of the prismatic compass, the sun compass and the big tank compass, and also how to navigate using the stars. The old 'Desert Rats' were always keen to show us that it was not as simple as it seemed, in order to impress upon the newly arrived 'Englishman' a proper sense of his ignorance. In fact, navigation is not so difficult provided one follows the rules and keeps calm.

One exercise involved a day of moving from point to point in a typically featureless area of the desert. In the evening my truck was bogged down in some soft sand and became absolutely immovable. There was nothing for it but to stay there all night and wait for the recovery vehicle. My driver had been in battle for a few days before an injury caused his return to base. I was glad to have as company a man with first-hand experience of the desert.

Although it is very hot during the day, desert nights are bitterly cold, even in July. The only way to keep warm was to fix the sand-mats round the front wheels and run the engine for twenty minutes, then switch it off and crawl underneath. This little tent was fairly comfortable, except for the oil which dripped at intervals on my face from the sump, three inches away. But even that was preferable to being frozen out in the open.

Suddenly the silence was broken by the sound of distant aircraft: the familiar drum-drumming of enemy planes. Soon there were flashes and explosions, some of the AA barrage defending one of the aerodromes outside Cairo, others of bombs dropping. The time between the flashes and explosions hung slowly in the air. When the raid, a short one, was over we crawled under the truck again and tried to sleep.

When dawn came we made a brew of tea, and waited for our rescuers. At about 9 a.m. I saw a figure walking slowly towards us; he was wearing no hat and swaying slightly. Realizing that he was a German, carrying an automatic pistol in his left hand, I told my driver to cover him with his rifle, and went forward. At about forty yards I drew my revolver and yelled, 'Halten! Hände hoch!' He dropped his automatic and put his left hand up, but seemed to be having difficulty with his right. Then I saw he was wounded, shot through the shoulder.

He was an airman, an observer, who had taken part in the raid we had watched. About twenty years old, fair-haired and blue-eyed, the classic Aryan type, he exuded Teutonic arrogance even in his present hopeless situation. Shot down by one of our fighters, his plane had crashed about three miles away, killing his crew. He had set out to walk to Cairo, but was actually going in the opposite direction.

Anxious to get medical treatment for his wound, he was most annoyed that we couldn't move our truck, and kept repeating, 'We go to Cairo, yes? We go now!' At length exhaustion made him sleep.

As we waited the sun became stronger and stronger, and mirages formed around us. I began to understand why men go mad when they're too long alone in a desert. All kinds of extraordinary thoughts came into my mind. When my driver went off for a stroll I sat in the passenger seat while the German airman slept in the shadow at the side. The heat haze lent an impression of unreality to everything, and strange fantasies began to slide through my mind. Thoughts of infinity twined themselves around scientific facts, and I found myself wondering whether the stars were wired in series or in parallel ... I remembered my days as a student in faraway, grey old Dublin, and the long, earnest philosophical and theological discussions we used to have by the fire in my rooms. And then, in contrast, I thought of my friend Richard, extrovert supreme, full of life in its truest sense, who was killed in Libya. As the two streams of thought crossed, some lines came, complete, into my head. I called them 'Discovery':

> Thomas sought the Infinite
> From a professorial Chair.
> All his life he pondered it,
> Pondered it, and sat on there.

> Richard thought the Infinite
> To be something of a bore.
> But in the desert he found it,
> Found it, and thought no more.

At about 2 p.m. a recovery vehicle arrived and towed the truck clear of the soft sand. We made our way back to Cairo with our prisoner as quickly as possible.

It was from base that the new recruit to the Middle East 'discovered' Cairo. As a rule he superficially judged the whole population from those with whom he came in contact: suffragis (servants), shopkeepers, touts, dragomen and gharry-drivers, and divided them into two classes, fools and knaves. The fools were those who tried to cheat you, but failed; the knaves were those who tried to cheat you, and succeeded. As the indigent majority relied on the overflowing pockets of tourists in peace-time and of soldiers in war-time, the grasping servility and lack of dignity among the lower classes was not unnatural.

Very few soldiers bothered to learn more of the language than some useful imperatives and patronizing nicknames. To start with, all taxi-drivers and menials were addressed as 'George'. On my first night I went by taxi into Cairo with another officer, whose name happened to be George. Every time I addressed him our driver turned round, grinned all over his face, and said, 'Yais, Sair? Yais!' We encouraged him to keep his eye on the road, despite his conviction that the conversation must be shared.

Words in common usage were: 'Igri!' – Hurry up! 'Esma!' – Come here! or Look out! 'Imshi!' – Get to hell out of here!' 'Mahlish!' – It doesn't matter. This last, used by the Egyptians rather than the English, referred to anything that could safely be referred to as unimportant – 'Put off till tomorrow what you can do today.' Perhaps your suffragi lost your best shirt, or burned a hole in the seat of your service dress trousers – 'Mahlish!' he would say with an ingratiating grin.

'Acker' was soldier slang for piastre; 'Wog' for a local inhabitant; and 'Mahfeesh' meant 'none' or 'no'. You might buy a packet of cigarettes for seven ackers and hand over a pound note; the Wog would accept it, wait until you'd opened the packet and lit up, then say, 'Mahfeesh change!'

Life at base was a welcome alternative to the monotony of soldiering in England during the period after Dunkirk, offering considerable variety, professionally as well as socially. On one occasion I was detailed to take 400 Italian prisoners of war to Suez by train. At 6 a.m. I paraded the escort, which consisted of a sergeant-major, three sergeants and thirty-five men, and marched immediately to the PoW camp. I had no idea how one went about a job like this and was relieved to discover that the Sergeant-Major had been on a similar party before.

At length the prisoners emerged in groups of fifty. The officer in charge of them gave me a slip of paper, which read:

1. Prisoners will not be allowed to converse with the local population.
2. While passing through towns prisoners will remain seated and the slatted blinds will be drawn.

'You shouldn't have much trouble with them,' he said, 'but they are fed up at leaving. They were given work here, and like to have some sort of regular occupation. Also, the Italian community in Cairo kept them well supplied with parcels through the Red Cross. So you may find one or two of them a bit bolshie – but, mahlish! Good luck!'

We set off along the dusty tree-lined roads with the prisoners marching in threes, carrying all their belongings. I led the column with a Military Policeman on each side of me, feeling almost like a prisoner myself being marched off to justice, and sharing the sense of there being no possible escape. The escort covered the flanks of the procession, which was about 250 yards long, and picturesque with the blue and white of the prisoners' uniforms. There were soldiers, sailors and airmen.

As we set off I could feel that the leading files were trying to rattle us by pushing up behind us as fast as they could.

'All right,' I said to the MPs, 'if they want to hurry we'll let 'em. Tired men are easier to handle than fresh ones.'

So we stepped out and it wasn't long before the braggadocio disappeared from their stride and they were shambling along, dropping their kit as they went.

The train was crowded and hot. I had all the slatted blinds drawn down and the stuffiness and the smell of overheated bodies became almost unendurable as we shunted around Cairo before finally steaming out into the desert, where the breeze from the train's movement made breathing tolerable.

There was something pathetic about these men. It was hard to think of them as enemies. They were like children, some mischievous and naughty, others doing all they could to show what good boys they really were. When at length I ordered the blinds and windows to be opened some of them thanked me as if I had conferred some special benefit upon them out of the goodness of my heart.

In view of the truculent behaviour of others I decided not to issue the rations till we reached our destination. The idea was a complete flop. No sooner had I announced my decision than they began to produce all sorts of foodstuffs from their kitbags: bars of chocolate, oranges, bananas, tinned fruit, biscuits, cakes. I could see the eyes of my escort sentries start out of their heads, especially when some of the dainties were wantonly flung out of the windows.

At last, to my relief, we steamed into Suez. A fresh escort was waiting for us, the prisoners were counted, handed over and signed for. This little ceremony intrigued me; in any organization, be it army, factory or village shop, a receipt is necessary whatever the nature of the goods.

For a few days after our return to Cairo we had the opportunity to sample the entertainments offered by that mysterious and sordid city. Soldiers being of necessity lonely men, these tended towards stimulation of the sexual urge, an urge which Axel Munthe maintained was nature's compensation for the reduction in population caused by pestilences and wars. The citizens of Cairo certainly cashed in on it.

Prostitutes employed a variety of touts to attract custom. Once, in broad daylight, a little boy of no more than six years old ran out from an alley-way, caught hold of my arm and said: "'Allo, Tanky officer! You like my sister, very clean, very cheap, very French!' The word 'French' was synonymous with 'chic'. In most cases it meant Syrian, Greek, Egyptian or any other Mediterranean nationality, mixed with a dash of French – anything from great-grandparent to mother or father.

Cairene night-clubs, noisy, smelly with cheap scent, garish, were like sticky fly-paper trapping the unwary into an expensive liaison with some dusky 'hostess'. As you entered, a proprietorial young lady, often extremely attractive, would seize your arm. The conversation would go something like this:

> 'Allo, darleeng! Je suis Georgette!
> You buy me drink? A cigarette?
> You are nice boy – we 'ave ze dance?
> Oh oui, bien sûr, I am from France!
>
> I am so dry – you buy champagne?
> Oh yais, yais please! We dance again?
> All right – it is too hot – too '*hot*'!
> Naughty boy! I like you a lot.
>
> Ah bon, champagne! Good 'ealth, cheero!
> Another, yais? Oh, where you go?
> Ah non, not yet, that is not right ...
> You come again tomorrow night?

Night-time in Cairo imposed a strain on the security forces and police, and squads were recruited to help. Before long my name appeared on the roster. This time I was given detailed instructions, instructions filling me with forebodings, which proved fully justified. I and the ten men under my command were to rendezvous with the military police at a hotel with the grandiose name of the King George V.

We approached through one of the drabbest quarters of the city, and pulled up at the shoddy building. Standing on the pavement was the red-cap (military policeman) who was to be our guide. He saluted, and led us into a large ground-floor room, bare of furniture except for some forms and four or five trestle tables.

"Ere we are, Sir. 'Ere's your guardroom for the night.'

'Thanks, Corporal.'

I mustered my men and explained our orders.

'Our job is to act as a reserve for the military police. If we are called out, it means it's something serious, that the MPs need help. Whatever happens you must stick together. Do not lose touch with each other. Now, I want you, Sergeant, and – let's see, who's the toughest here – ah, yes, you'll do! If there's trouble you two will stick by me and see that I don't get hit! As you know, striking an officer is a very serious offence in the army, so you've got to – er – sort of protect these chaps against themselves by protecting me. Personally, I think it's a damn good idea ... '

The men were grinning, so I knew I was lucky tonight. I'd been given a first-class lot.

'Right, now I want you to divide into pairs and keep together in any rough-house. Remember, today is pay-day, so trouble is likely. OK? No questions?'

I went outside to warn the driver of the truck that he must be ready to move off at a moment's notice. I let the men go in pairs to the services canteen across the way, and stood outside watching the strange procession that nightly haunted a Cairo street. Soldiers and airmen back from the desert for a few days' leave; Egyptian soldiers, smart in tunic and fez; street vendors offering lemonade, water and trinkets; lithe dusky women with dark eyes, some going about their lawful occasions, others waiting to pounce on willing but unwary soldiers; and in the background a distant tintinnabulation of music from the cabarets and dance-halls. The theme under-lying these variations was poverty – stinking and disease-ridden, such poverty as only the East knows, and, having nothing to contrast it with, accepts without shame.

Darkness fell. The red-cap, who was in a sense my ADC, started up.

'Look, Sir! Someone's after that boy!'

There was a white streak, and I could make out in the dark centre of the street a fleeting figure racing away as though all the demons in hell were after him. A soldier was in pursuit, but he gave up suddenly and disappeared into the shadows. By now a crowd was chasing the robed fugitive, followed by the red-cap and four of my men.

I waited by the truck until a surge of voices coming towards me announced that the MP had made his capture.

'Where's the boy, Corporal?' I asked.

'Here, Sir,' he answered without a smile, indicating his prisoner, a venerable-looking Egyptian about sixty years old.

'Well, what's the matter?'

'Says he was attacked by some soldiers in a café up the street, Sir.'

'Right, we'll investigate. Bring him along.'

The café was empty except for three soldiers sitting at one table, and a Rhodesian sergeant-major at another. As we entered, one of the men stood up. He was about six foot four inches tall. He took a menacing pace towards the Egyptian, who, trapped by the Corporal's grip and the crush of curious spectators behind him, went grey and struggled futilely.

'You here again, you – '

'Sit down!' I roared.

He hesitated, then sat down.

'What's the trouble?'

'Well, Sir, it's like this. We was sitting here quiet like, talking, and this bugger was behind the bar, when he comes pestering us and insulting my regiment – '

'No, Sah! No, Sah!' the Egyptian broke in shrilly. 'I only try sell soldier watch – very good watch – look, Sah!' He produced about a dozen watches from the folds of his galabeah. 'Very good watch, Sah!' A pause. 'You buy watch, Sah? Very good – '

'No, thank you. Was this man selling drinks when he was behind the bar?'

'Don't know wot 'e was doing, Sir – you see we ain't been drinking – but 'e comes up 'ere and insults my regiment.'

He picked up his beret, displaying the badge of a distinguished cavalry regiment renowned for its work in the desert.

'Best regiment in the desert, Sir, and I won't 'ave it insulted!'

The man was getting worked up again. Realizing that despite his assurances he was distinctly tight, I decided that the best thing was to close the incident at once.

'Yes,' I said, 'I know your regiment, and you're quite right. *You* know it's the best regiment in the desert, and *I* know it's the best regiment in the desert – what the hell does it matter what a bloke like this thinks? Suppose we forget it. And I don't expect to hear anything more from you tonight. OK?'

'OK, Sir. And thanks.'

He stood up and to my surprise shook me enthusiastically by the hand. His companions followed suit. One of them, a diminutive creature with a wizened desert-brown face, pointed at my cap badge and said, 'I know your lot, Sir, worked with 'em in France.' With that he saluted, hatless, belched, and abruptly collapsed onto his chair.

'Right, Corporal,' I said, 'let the Egyptian go, and advise him not to come up this street again.'

Walking back with my men, I tried to imagine a scene like that taking place in some English city. Out here there was a difference in the relationship between officer and man: less formality, more confidence and, in the end, a finer if less obvious discipline.

While I was ruminating, a military police car drew up in front of me. A sergeant got out and saluted.

'We're closing the "New Cairo" cabaret, Sir. Would you bring your men along?'

He indicated a large, brightly lit building across the road.

'OK, Sergeant. How do you intend to set about it?'

'We've told the proprietor to start the band on "God Save the King". While they're playing we'll slip in the back door – and we want your chaps to block the entrance in case of trouble.'

I thought of the six-foot-plus cavalryman we had just dealt with and tried not to be too impressed at the prospect of blocking the door against twenty or so as big as him, and certainly more drunk.

'"God Save the King", Sergeant? Will that keep them quiet?'

'Oh yes, Sir. Mostly Commonwealth troops. Very loyal.'

'Right. Let's get moving.'

We went across into the foyer. The concluding strains of the national anthem blared, none too victoriously, I thought, through a door on the left. I posted two men by the outer entrance, with instructions not to let anyone else in, and two others at the inner door within sight of the first pair. The remainder followed me inside.

The place was packed with British, Canadian, Australian and French troops. I had a vivid sense of having walked into a theatre at a point of intense drama. The band was playing with vigour, and obvious nervousness, apparently ready at any moment to throw down their instruments and run for their lives.

The rest of the room presented a scene of unreal immobility. Incongruously among the wrecked chairs and tables, broken glasses and upturned bottles, some fifty soldiers of various nationalities stood to attention while the anthem was played. Most were singing lustily, while a few gripped friends or pillars as they endeavoured to remain upright. At the far end of the room, by the stage, a rabble of terrified women clutched their skirts to keep them clear of the pools of beer on the floor.

I glanced round and saw the red caps of the MPs as they stood in the doorways and alcoves. Under the peaks was that stony look which all policemen wear when they are on the job. I sensed that the situation was now in hand.

As the anthem ceased the greater part of the crowd picked up caps and strolled with exaggerated nonchalance towards the doors. The few obstinate groups remaining were firmly, but quite kindly, ushered out by the MPs.

I rounded up my men and we set off back to headquarters.

'Must 'ave been quite a party before we got there, Sir,' one of the men remarked. 'Could've been nasty. Cor, I could do with a cuppa now. 'Ope we don't 'ave any more excitements!'

'I'm afraid we do,' I replied.

Outside the hotel stood a three-ton lorry, from which an extraordinary noise was coming – reminiscent of feeding-time at a zoo. A smaller vehicle, with MP markings, was parked behind. As we arrived six MPs dismounted and placed themselves in a semicircle behind the three-tonner. The Major in charge shouted to me above the strange raucous din, 'You're to look after this lot, Lieutenant!'

'What lot?' I asked, stupid with shock. He ignored me and gave a signal to his sergeant. The back of the lorry was let down, and steps set in place. Down these scrambled a swarm of women, shrieking, gesticulating, cursing. Arms flailed, stockinged legs flashed in the garish light. With abrupt, rugged efficiency, the MPs herded them into my guardroom. Dumb with apprehension I followed.

'Now,' said the Major, who had the manner of a man whose occupation permits no play of humour or compassion, 'keep these women here until you get further orders. In about an hour's time, when the Egyptian police are ready for them, you will take them to the police barracks and hand them over. There are twenty-three of them – sign for them here, please – and twenty-three will be expected at the barracks, so see you get them there. And don't forget to get a receipt. Understood?'

'Yes, Sir. But who are they?'

'Who are they? Who the hell do you think they are? Tarts, of course!'

'Well, yes, I'd sort of gathered that. But I didn't know we had the right to arrest them.'

'Just look at 'em,' he said grimly, 'look at that one over there!'

He pointed out a dark-skinned creature who must have been at least fifty years old. Her skin was grey and eaten with disease. One brownish fang protruded over her lower lip, and her eyes, which once might have been beautiful, exuded a yellow gum.

'From the Arab Quarter,' explained the Major briskly, as though he were reading from a report. 'Caught soliciting – a crime in these parts, though you mightn't think it. We work with the Egyptian authorities in this matter. Can you imagine the trade mark she'd leave on some drunken soldier? Well, you have your orders. See you later.'

'One moment, Sir! How do I get them to the barracks?'

'A vehicle will be sent, and a squad of my men. I may come myself if I'm free. But the responsibility is yours.'

When he left, the women seemed to sense a departure of authority. Erupting into fresh outbursts they rushed towards the door. I moved quickly across, and my men formed a barrier in front of it. For fully a minute I was surrounded and crushed. The smell was nauseating, a thick mixture of unclean bodies and back-street scent. It was a humiliating position for a newly commissioned officer, whose imagination had foreshadowed battles of a more dramatic nature. My temper flared through my disgust, and I flung the nearest woman back against the others, pushed myself clear and jumped onto a table.

'Get back!' I yelled. 'Get back to the other end of the room!'

There was a sudden silence. 'Now look,' I said, trying to sound authoritative yet reasonable, 'you're here, and there's nothing you or I can do about it. If you behave – '

At this there was a concerted scream, and they rushed the table. There was only one thing for it. I drew my revolver.

The women stood still, gaping and wordless. The smell of fear was added to the other odours, and dusky skins turned pale brown. The white girls, the 'very French', stood out in the harsh light of the uncovered bulbs, their make-up hideous as it became dislodged with sweat.

In this heroic posture I surveyed my prisoners. They moved slowly to the other end of the room and huddled onto benches, abject, mumbling incoherently. Then I heard a strange, chilling sound. A wailing, tearful screech, composed half of misery and half of anger, it started at one side of the crowd and spread with a sickening crescendo to the other side.

'Fair breaks yer 'eart,' I heard one of my men mutter. I glanced down at him. He had sparked a feeling that I had deliberately been stifling – pity. I understood now the emotion-less set of the Major's face. These raddled wrecks, I thought, they're human, aren't they, with the same rights as other humans to dignity and respect? Once they must have had hopes of life, once been loved; and perhaps were loved even now. Were there children to be fed, old people to be kept alive, somehow? What right had we – I – to herd them like cattle in a pen? In the sight of God all souls are equal. But in the sight of generals these women were a source of disease, and therefore of casualties, to the forces. I made a conscious effort to suppress my feelings, but could not eradicate one of blind emptiness and mechanical action, which I imagine is that of an execu-tioner at the final moment.

'It fair breaks yer 'eart!' the man repeated.

'Yer right,' said another voice ruefully, 'it's put me off women for life!'

An hour passed, an uneasy hour of embarrassed tension interrupted by sobs. Then the telephone rang.

'Have your lady friends ready,' said the Major. 'We'll be along in five minutes.'

The journey was less eventful than I had feared. The Major led in a jeep, followed by the three-tonner with its pathetic cargo; behind this came the MPs, and finally myself and my men.

We drove into a high-walled yard where a squad of Egyptian

police stood ready. The ladies were unloaded and counted, and I was given my receipt. As soon as the Egyptians took over, the prisoners started screaming and hitting out again. The treatment they received from the police was far from chivalrous. Gradually the noise subsided as the procession struggled out of sight into the dark passages of the prison.

Our tour of duty was almost completed. All that remained was the formality of making my report at military police headquarters. We followed the Major's jeep through quiet brooding streets in the thin golden light before dawn.

In the Major's office, we sat down with his desk between us. He handed me a sheet of paper.

'Write your report on that.'

I stared at it. A whole sheet of foolscap, white and empty, which at any normal time would have been inviting, now oppressed me with its very largeness. I was tired, and the sight of all this space filled me with mental agoraphobia. No words would come. At last, feeling inadequate and stupid, I asked how much detail I should include. He looked up from what he was writing, a frown drawing his brows together.

'*De*tail? How much *de*tail?' He emphasized the first syllable most unpleasantly. '*De*tail? Just put "Nothing to report."'

The Free French

Tension rose in Cairo with the rumours that Rommel was mounting a great offensive, and that soon Egypt would be overrun by the Germans. Pro-Nazis and Fascists among the population became more active, and the military police periodically put the city out of bounds without warning, confining all service personnel to barracks. A number of enemy agents in British uniforms were captured on these occasions.

The evacuation of civilians and of some of the Women's Services increased this tension. Convoys passed through the streets, troop carriers, guns, tanks under tarpaulins on transporters, RAF vehicles – endless reinforcements of equipment (some of it new and secret), and cheerful, grinning troops off to 'The Blue'. Obviously something was happening, or going to happen, up there in the desert.

Then, on 31 August 1942, Rommel attacked. His intention was to break through the Alamein Line, destroy the Eighth

Army, reach Cairo and Alexandria, and secure the delta. He
was opposed by the new Army Commander, General Bernard
Montgomery, who had inherited the dispositions organized so
brilliantly by his predecessor, General Auchinleck, after the retreat from Gazala. The main thrust was directed against the
southern sector. Two German and two Italian armoured divisions drove eastward, then northward towards the Alam Halfa
Ridge. Monty had foreseen this tactic and decided on his response, as he recalled in his memoirs: 'We would fight a static
battle and my forces would not move; his tanks would come
up against our tanks in hull-down positions at the western
edge of the Alam Halfa Ridge.'

In the 'corridor' thus formed, hindered by soft sand, lack of
fuel and the attentions of the RAF, Rommel's drive came to a
halt. Above all, his tanks suffered heavy casualties from the
dug-in British armour. His retreat marked the turning-point in
the Middle Eastern war. Monty had won his first desert battle
in convincing style. Whatever criticisms may with hindsight be
levelled against him for not following up this victory, the fact
is that he needed time to forge the Eighth Army into a great
weapon; and his vindication is that it became invincible.

I expected that all this excitement would mean an immediate
posting to the desert. Instead I was posted to HQ BTE. At this
stage BTE was still an operational HQ, charged with defending
the delta, a role it retained until Monty ordered that the defence
of the cities of Egypt would be 'fought out *here* at Alamein'.

BTE, which was housed in the Semiramis Hotel on the east
bank of the Nile, commanded divisions of many nationalities:
Indian, British, Australian and French. My job was Liaison
Officer to the 1st Free French Brigade under General Koenig,
which was resting after its magnificent defence of Bir Hakim.

Their HQ was some eleven miles out of Cairo on the Suez
road. I used to ride out there once a day with despatches on a
terrifyingly powerful Norton motorbike. I received them at
noon, and was in the Brigade-Major's tent about half an hour
later.

The atmosphere in any officers' mess – whatever the nationality – is basically the same. Customs differ, but there is a
common sense of tradition, as well as a camaraderie and defer-
ence to rank. But in this mess, due to the artificial situation, the

atmosphere was unique. Historically France is a military nation with a deep-rooted pride in its forces. The humiliation of 1940 left it bewildered and sometimes, as compensation, truculent. Much of its insecurity stemmed from the split between those who accepted the German-dominated Vichy government, and those who followed de Gaulle to form the Free French Forces overseas. Each group was suspicious of the intentions of the other, and aware of the distrust in which they were held by the British and their allies.

The cruelty of this dilemma was brought home to me in conversation with the Brigade-Major. He had come over to the Free French from the Vichy forces in Syria, but only after lengthy soul-searching. For many French people the situation seemed less clear-cut than it did to us, and, given these divisions in loyalty, it was understandable that Allied Intelligence should try to determine the sincerity of a man's switch from one side to the other. For this reason the despatches conveyed frequently omitted information of a top-secret quality. The French were conscious of this, resented it, and sometimes treated me as though I were the author of these despatches.

On the surface there was considerable *bonhomie*. The Brigade-Major used to take me over to the mess tent to discuss our business over a bottle of beer. Then he would press me to stay for lunch. It was August, and the hottest part of the day, yet the meal was on the fullest scale, and accompanied by beer, wine and liqueurs. I wondered if this emphasis on alcohol was not designed to trap me into some injudicious slip of the tongue. As I was nothing more than a very junior harbinger, my mind pleasantly blank of military secrets, I was able to enjoy this hospitality without inhibition.

General Koenig sat at the head of the table cracking jokes in a dry, even voice. He enjoyed my discomfort when on one occasion I politely – and loudly – joined in the laughter, not realizing its esoteric nature, which excluded any foreigner from understanding it.

I became fascinated by this man, about whom legends were already beginning to form. Forty-four years of age, in the prime of life, he immediately conveyed an impression of alertness, of a thoughtful, calculating mind. To the French community he was the Hero of Bir Hakim. In the spring of 1942 the

Eighth Army was on a line stretching roughly 30 miles south-eastwards from Gazala to Bir Hakim, a fortified oasis held by the 1st Free French Brigade. The British intention was to launch an offensive from this position, but unfortunately Rommel struck first, on 22 May. Being designed for attack rather than defence, the British dispositions lacked depth.

As Rommel began to drive the Eighth Army back in the centre, he sent a strong force to outflank Bir Hakim. In his own description of the battle he wrote: 'On the night 1–2 June 90 Light Division and the Trieste [Division] moved against Bir Hakim. They crossed the minefield without heavy casualties, thus shutting off the fortress from the east.' Bir Hakim was now encircled. Rommel went on:

The Trieste from the north-east and 90 Light from the south-east advanced against the fortifications ['a network of slit trenches and pill-boxes', Liddell Hart], field positions and minefields of the French defenders. With our preliminary barrage there began a battle of extraordinary severity, which was to last ten whole days. I frequently took over command of the assault forces myself and seldom in Africa was I given such a hard-fought battle.

The story is completed by Liddell Hart in *The Tanks*:

On the evening of the 10th, one of [Rommel's] battle-groups broke into the French defences, and it became clear that the end was near. So during the night, the garrison evacuated the 'box' – in accord with Ritchie's instructions – although they had to leave much of their equipment behind. Most of them managed to slip away under cover of darkness. That was just in time, for Rommel was bringing down the rest of the 15th Panzer Division to seal the ring.

Rommel, however, profited on balance from the fall of Bir Hakim. He had cleared away an awkward obstacle, and was now free to concentrate all his German troops for a decisive blow against an opponent who was rather disorganized and precariously spread ...

In June 1940 Marie-Pierre Koenig had been evacuated to England, where he became a leading commander of de Gaulle's Free French Forces. After the destruction of the Axis forces in North Africa he was the French representative on Eisenhower's HQ, and before the end of the war he commanded the French Army in Germany. He was Defence Minister in France in 1954 and 1955.

That is a potted history of the career of a remarkable man. Set out like that it seems conventional enough; but it was a just success for this brilliant opportunist. It was totally in character that in 1944 he was Director of Resistance in Occupied France.

FOUR

The Desert

At last our postings came through and we were sent up to the desert. I was among a small group which joined the 3rd Battalion, The Royal Tank Regiment, then in a training area west of the Wadi Natrun. We were met by the Adjutant, Guy Barker, who gave us a brief history of the battalion since the beginning of the war. They were in the rearguard at Calais in 1940 and, when reformed, arrived in the Middle East just in time for the disastrous Greek expedition. Forced to abandon their tanks, they were evacuated to Crete, and suffered as targets for the *Luftwaffe* and the German paratroops for a frustrating few weeks. In early 1942 they fought in the abortive campaign in the Western Desert and, recently equipped with the new American Grant tanks, played a major part in the delaying action at Gazala. Finally, following a distinguished contribution to victory at Alam Halfa, they had been withdrawn to their present position to rest and refit.

Next morning we were interviewed by the CO, Lt Col H.E. (Pete) Pyman. Dark, short, supremely self-assured, he strutted into the tent and sat down facing us across a trestle-table. He placed his fingertips together in a mannerism reminiscent of a priest at prayer except for the way he drummed them together. This was the only sign of his dynamic energy, otherwise he personified self-control.

In profile and stature Pyman was not unlike Napoleon, a fact of which I suspected he was well aware. I got the impression that he had a sense of humour, but that this was reserved for off-duty occasions, and he rarely considered himself off duty.

After a rather more detailed history of the battalion, and a résumé of the Principles of War, he put his elbows on the table, tapped the tips of his fingers together with extra vigour to emphasize his words, and said: 'There are *three* things I will not tolerate in my officers. Drunkenness – idleness – and stupidity.' He turned to the Adjutant. 'Anything else, Guy?' Guy could think of nothing else that his chief would not tolerate, so we were despatched to our respective squadrons.

I went to 'A' Squadron, then under command of the famous Bob Crisp, journalist, writer, and South African Test cricketer. Bob, at the time the only officer below field rank to have been awarded the DSO, was already a legend in the desert. He had the quality of an Elizabethan buccaneer, and was in fact a bit piratical by nature. He loved to command, but did not like taking orders. Pete Pyman's strict discipline did not suit Bob, who could never resist attacking the enemy, and had in previous battles detached himself and his tanks to do so. Such sorties, while spectacular and sometimes of limited success, could only weaken the battalion.

To me Bob was peerless. My hero-worship was engendered not only by his military adventures and expertise at cricket, but also by his love of poetry. That first night in the squadron mess tent he quoted passages from Shakespeare with a sensitivity and passion that enthralled me.

His cricketing career was brilliant. He could swing the ball either way and, bringing it down from a good height, make it lift awkwardly. In England in 1935 he took 107 wickets (19.58), including 13 in the five tests. He twice took four wickets in four balls, once for Western Province against Griqualand in 1931/32, and once against Natal in 1933/34. He had great courage and determination; in the 1935 test at Trent Bridge, when Maurice Leyland and Bob Wyatt were in command at the crease in a record stand, Bob limped off the field with a foot inflamed from a blood blister. The doctor warned him not to bowl again that day but he returned to take the wickets of both batsmen.

He had a dry and sometimes macabre sense of humour, which was at its sharpest during battle, as was his deep compassion for his officers and men.

I was lucky in being given command of the Recce (Reconnaissance) Troop, whose role was possibly the most interesting and exciting in the battalion. The men were carefully picked for the job, which required quick thinking, accurate navigation and first-class reporting. We were equipped with minute Daimler scout cars, known as dingoes. These had the fluid fly-wheel, which made them particularly well suited to the sandy surfaces, and were heavily armoured, but had no armament except a Bren gun issued by the Quartermaster when he had any to spare. Only one in two cars had a wireless. The estab-lishment was ten cars, divided into five patrols of two each, but at no time did I have more than seven cars.

When the battalion advanced we moved in a crescent formation in front of the leading squadron, sometimes a few yards ahead, sometimes up to 500 yards, depending on the features of the ground and the battle situation. We were the eyes of the battalion, or its antennae, seeking to establish contact with the enemy, report his positions and if possible his strength. Often we discovered the former when we drew his fire. Then, as I made my report on the air, we withdrew as fast as we could behind the tanks, to wait there until needed again.

I inherited this small but exciting command from an officer who had led the troop with outstanding success for the last six months. I could sense the men's disappointment that this 'pale face' from Blighty, who had never been in battle, was to take over. It was going to be hard to establish myself as their leader, but my training as an officer had a much wider application than that of the other ranks, which in essence was merely to obey orders, and I had the advice and experience of a number of outstanding officers to draw on.

We spent six weeks training in that patch of desert. Exercise after exercise, day in day out, practising the same things all the time until we could do them in our sleep. Yet it was never good enough for the CO. Pete was a perfectionist, determined that his battalion would perform as a machine-like weapon, making the maximum contribution and cutting casualties to a minimum.

Our main exercise was to learn how to go through a mine-field at night and fan out into battle positions at dawn. The sappers cleared gaps and lighted the verges, putting empty petrol-tins, with a tiny cross-shaped slit in one side, on stakes about three feet high; the light inside was visible to us but not to the enemy. Then the fighting vehicles crossed, followed by the echelon. The whole regimental group had to pass through, and in those days there were no 'Priests' (tracked vehicles for pulling artillery), so the 25-pounders were always sticking in soft sand, the quads not being powerful enough to pull them out. The infantry vehicles, too, were underpowered, as were those of our own echelon, but, whatever the difficulties, Pete insisted that the column must keep going. A drill was at last devised whereby tanks towed 25-pounders and anti-tank guns. Later, the sweat, tedium and fatigue of those weeks resulted in the enemy's shock at our speed in crossing his minefields.

When daylight came the battalion and supporting troops would be in battle positions, ready to practise an advance or a withdrawal. At first we did squadron schemes, then regimental, then brigade. It was collective training on a grand scale.

A regimental group on the move in battle formation in the desert was a thrilling sight. In front was my Recce troop, moving from ridge to ridge ahead of the light squadron – in those days Crusaders, like lean destroyers, a thin grey line covering the battalion front. Behind them, forming opposite sides of a square, lumbered the two heavy squadrons, composed of Grants; in the centre was RHQ, with the 25-pounders on one side and the infantry in carriers on the other; and in the rear, forming the fourth side of the square, the 'soft' vehicles of the echelon. The tanks threw up trails of sand and from a distance looked like fast ships at sea laying a smoke-screen. On each wireless mast fluttered a small coloured pennant. The drill was perfect by the end of these six weeks, and I always felt exhilarated when we moved, flat out, in this formation across an even stretch of sand.

At one point, the Recce troop would report an imaginary contact with the enemy. The Crusaders advanced to confirm, to cover my dingoes, and to engage if need be. Gradually a picture was built up from which the CO could deduce what sort of opposition he had met, and dispose his squadrons, gunners and infantry accordingly. I learnt a lot from these reports. Never having seen an enemy gun position, I now heard descriptions from people who had, and soon found I knew where to expect one, and could give reasonable-sounding reports myself.

One morning I went out to take a fitter to a vehicle that had broken down during an exercise. We reached it at midday but the job took longer than expected and dusk fell as we returned to the battalion. A mist came up, reducing visibility to thirty yards. At first I thought I must have made a mistake in my calculations, for by my reckoning we should have been on the outskirts of our squadron area. I decided to continue for another mile, and proceeded, with the repaired vehicle lumbering along uncomfortably behind. Then I heard a low drumming sound. We halted and switched off the engine, listening. It seemed to be coming from all sides, a deep, monotonous burr-burr, throbbing through the darkness.

'Tanks,' said my driver, 'something's up.'

We advanced again until we made out the black shape of a Crusader. The commander, a sergeant, was standing in the turret, muffled, shivering, with the earphones over his head. He recognized us and shouted: 'Moving in ten minutes!'

'What – the whole battalion?'

'Yes.'

I felt stunned. Here was the moment we had all been waiting for, training for, and it had come upon me unawares. I directed the rescued vehicle to the echelon, and made off to Squadron HQ.

'Ah, here he is,' said Bob, sounding as unconcerned as if I'd never left the area and was merely a few minutes late. 'Look, here are your maps. We move any moment now. You and your troop will follow Squadron HQ. OK?'

'No, Sir, not really. I haven't been able to see my troop since I got back, so I don't know whether they're teed up or topped up or anything. In case you move before we're ready, can you give me the bearing?'

'270 degrees for three miles, then further orders will be issued.' Due west, in fact.

I found my troop prepared and set to move, as might have been expected. The cars were all packed and a thoughtful corporal had got my personal kit ready. There remained the problem of the spare crews; a 30-cwt truck had been provided, but it was practically full when it arrived. The men were in despair.

'It's impossible, Sir, we can't all get onto this with our kit.'

I felt the same desperate helplessness surging up in me.

'Nonsense, Corporal,' I snapped, trying to sound Napoleonic, 'nothing's impossible! Throw the bedding on first and then climb on yourselves. It won't be comfortable, but it's either that or staying here – in which case you die of starvation. Go on, get cracking!'

To my surprise and relief the impossible was achieved. The truck lurched off into the night with its disgruntled cargo, looking as though it would capsize at any moment.

At length I drove up to SHQ followed by my six other little cars. Two minutes later the column moved off.

The Alamein Line

Everything had happened so quickly that I was completely out of the picture, with no idea of where we were going or what we were going to do when we got there. The only clue was that we were starting in a due westerly direction. Obviously it wasn't another scheme, because the whole battalion was moving and not just the fighting vehicles. Perhaps Rommel had broken through and we were going to block the gap.

Next morning we were shown our route and told that we were to take over a sector in the Alamein Line.

Two days later we halted in open leaguer. I was sent forward with the Assistant Adjutant to recce the route and make arrangements with the battalion whose area we were taking over. We found them in a wadi known as Fly Valley. A fierce battle there at the end of August had resulted in heavy casualties on both sides. Swarms of flies infested the place, fat greedy flies fed on human corpses. As soon as you opened a tin of bully beef the part exposed to the air was covered at once with a black nauseating mass.

We stayed there overnight, marking on our maps the position of every tank and the best routes for our own squadrons to approach. Then we returned and led the battalion into the new area by night. Each tank went to a spot evacuated by one of the other battalion. We were told that we had three days to rest, that we must eat and sleep as much as possible, and keep movement to a minimum, as this was all part of a huge plan to fox the enemy. Several of his recce planes did come over but failed to notice that we had moved in.

During these days I came to know my troop better and to appreciate their comradeship and loyalty. We knew that there was a big show coming off but for security reasons the plan was not yet disclosed to us. Unlike me, the men had been through all this before, yet wanted the reassurance that they had a leader. The fact, therefore, that I had not yet been in battle meant nothing now; we were simply a group of men about to share danger together, and the only way to do this with confidence was to support and trust each other.

My driver, Trooper Johnston from Liverpool, was one of the outstanding characters in the battalion. His self-assurance, whether when 'rolling' our car successfully over a treacherous patch of soft sand or fiddling the rations ('You see, Sir, I always thinks one step ahead of the other man'), was startling to one of my inexperience. Brown-haired, high-cheek-boned, with the compact build and coordinated movements of an athlete, Johnston combined cynicism and immaturity. I fully believed him when he told me that his object was to win the VC, and since this award is so often given posthumously, and he and I shared a small vehicle with him at the controls, I acknowledged the ambition with no enthusiasm.

To me his worth lay in his brilliant handling of my car (he had trained as a test driver before the war) and his stimulating nature – life was never flat with Johnston around.

Two of my car commanders were lance-corporals who would have held higher rank in a tank troop. They had refused promotion because they wanted to remain together and because they liked the Recce troop, where the establishment for NCOs was already complete. One of these, Bennett, was a north-country townsman with a remarkably agile brain, who expressed his socialistic views with clarity and conviction. The fact that they conflicted with my own opinions never impeded my confidence in his loyalty and initiative. Lance-Corporal Beck was his opposite in every respect. Bennett represented the 'civilian' type of NCO; Beck was a regular soldier, unimaginative but intelligent, and incomparably efficient at routine work. They made a perfect team, around whose enthusiasm was built the spirit of this troop.

During these few days we had our main meal in the evening, when there were fewer flies. Much thought went into the preparation of these meals. A menu was submitted to me during the day, ostensibly for my approval, but in reality for my mystification. It would contain such items as burgoo,

panhaggelty and scowse, and I was expected to exclaim my
ignorance of what they were. Then I was treated to a long
dissertation, not only about the dish, but about the locality in
which it was a speciality. It was an expression of the men's
nostalgia for home and the people who made these dishes for
them in better times.

After the meals – so well prepared despite the improvisation
necessary – we sat in a circle and talked. Photos were produced
out of grubby pay-books and handed round. Comment was
always frank, and I was amazed at the good humour with
which some remarks were taken. Bert was one of the drivers, a
quaint, undersized gnome who, being nearly forty, had no
right to be in the fighting echelon. But he had joined up from
the Durham mines to have a crack at the Hun, and nothing
would induce him to take a job further back. He handed me a
photo of his wife, a fine, strongly built, kindly-faced woman,
head and shoulders taller than her Bert. I made suitable comments, which seemed to please him, and passed it on to my
neighbour.

'A proper battleship, Bert,' he said. 'I bet she gives you a
rough time in bed!'

'She's all right,' he grinned reminiscently, contented that
through this conversation a link was established with his
adored, comfortable woman away back in Durham.

The men talked unselfconsciously about themselves, their
families, their ambitions, the government, the enemy –
everything under the sun, in conversations which drew us
together as a team. A week later Bert's car was blown up on a
mine and his commander killed. Unhurt, but badly shaken, he
was carried over to my car, where we made him a brew of tea.
His passion was strong tea, 'so as the spoon will stand up in it!'
I handed him the mug and said, 'Here you are, Bert, drink this
if you can – the spoon jumped right out of it!' He gave me a
grin that was almost conspiratorial, so close was the rapport
between us.

Eventually we moved off again, by night. I was leading
since I had recced the route the day before. Through our own
minefield gaps we went, winding along tortuous tracks, nose
to tail, slowly, the Recce troops followed by the Crusaders,
then RHQ, the Grants, and finally the new Shermans. We

followed 'Hat' track till we came to our area, where the camouflage scheme which so completely outwitted the enemy was in evidence. Great 'sun-shields', frames in the shape of three-ton lorries, lay dotted about. Each tank was driven up to one, the crew dismantled the sun-shield and re-erected it over the tank. Then for two hours we laboured to obliterate the tracks of the tanks before daylight.

Over the next two days, the remainder of the brigade and an infantry division moved into the area. Pete called a conference and told us the plan. On 23 October, tomorrow, the barrage would begin. The guns would be thirty yards apart and stretch from the sea to the Qattara Depression. A full-scale attack would be mounted in the southern sector, but that was a feint to draw off the enemy's armour. The real thrust was in the north, where we were to be. The infantry would go in first, followed by the tanks, which would fan out beyond the mine-fields.

He stopped talking and looked at each of us for a moment as we sat silent on the sand. Then he lifted his head, and said, as though to himself, 'It's a beautiful plan,' a semi-smile of appreciation relieving his stern features.

We returned to our troops and passed on the information. The men were quiet as they sat eating their lunch. As veterans they could be relied on thoroughly to prepare themselves and their equipment for battle. But also as veterans they knew that the longer you go on fighting the shorter become the odds on your being hit. Occasionally I was asked questions and it wasn't long before Johnston, whisking a little cloud of flies off his food, said, 'What's our job, Sir? I mean, we're Recce, and we won't be much use until we get moving after the break-through.'

'Oh, I think the CO will find something for us to do,' I replied as nonchalantly as I could. 'Perhaps he'll use us as observation posts.'

'You mean as bloody targets, don't you?'

I ignored the insolence, which, although in character, was here the product of nerves; as I was not immune to them myself I felt I might over-react if I spoke at all.

The rest of the day, after our stint of maintenance, was spent writing and (in my case) censoring letters, and rereading old ones.

I could not sleep that night, twisting and turning in my sleeping-bag, trying to shape the sand to fit my body. Life had suddenly become very precious. I thought back to things I had taken for granted, commonplace things like sitting in an arm-chair in mid-winter, reading. My mind flitted across isolated, unconnected incidents: children's parties with Musical Chairs, the breathless silence when the music stopped and wide-open eyes looked to see which of us was 'out'; my hat blowing off in Regent Street and being flattened by a bus; the journey from Waterloo to start my first job, feeling nervous and very much alone; sailing on Mulroy Bay in Donegal with Reginald Osborne the day war was declared; and, most poignantly, the day I said goodbye to my parents.

I wondered what would happen when the battle started. Would I want to run away? Would my mind be paralysed with fear, and my men regard me with contempt?

I looked up at the sky. The deathly desert stillness perme-ated the night like something positive. There were guns firing very far away: an irrelevant noise, like dogs barking on some distant farm. It was bright and starry. A long, ribbed, cigar-shaped cloud moved across the moon and, as it came over-head, disintegrated into a herring-bone pattern, a long series of gradually separating Vs. An omen, I thought, and felt ridicu-lously, illogically happy.

The Great Battle

At last light on 23 October we formed up again on the 'Hat' track. This time my troop was behind 'A' Squadron HQ. As the long, growling column wound off into the night and the flying dust, I experienced a sense of relief: the preparations were finished and the adventure was on.

We passed medical stations, Pioneers maintaining the track, groups of military police, traffic control points. Everyone was busy, everyone gave us the V sign.

At last what we had all been waiting for began. At ten o'clock, a mile ahead, the blackness was lit up from horizon to horizon with innumerable white and crimson flashes, which merged to become one long flickering glow of blood-red light. The barrage had begun! We grinned at each other and waited for the reverberation of the explosions. The column speeded up and the sound of the cannonade, like some titanic Bren gun, roared louder and louder as we approached. Finally we passed right through the line of guns, our ears splitting, and halted, with the head of the column on Springbok Road.

I had instructions to patrol forward from this point as far as the enemy minefields. As we set off amid the din of the guns and the satanic fairyland of tracer bullets, shells and Very lights, I felt an extraordinary, irrational elation, a surrender to the resounding majesty of battle.

A searchlight was directed up from each corner of the square, so that our planes would not confuse our positions with those of the enemy. Strangely, as I advanced with the second car close behind mine, the noise diminished, even though we were now in front of the guns. We passed an advanced dressing station and I stopped to speak to the commanding officer, realizing that the noise had not really decreased but had deafened me, for I could not hear what the MO was saying.

But I did hear Johnston, who yelled, 'Look out, Sir!' The sand was ripped up in a series of spouts some fifteen yards away, by shells or small bombs, and I decided to proceed on our mission at once.

We went on through another minefield that the sappers were lighting. When challenged, I identified myself and asked if the gap would be ready for the battalion. They said it would, but to keep the tracks on the left and the wheels on the right.

A few hundred yards further on we reached our objective, the German minefield. It was not lighted. Suddenly I saw movement in the gap. Emerging slowly from the gloom was the dark form of a tank. For a moment fear chilled my body and my mind. Against this monster we were helpless; and wireless silence meant I could not warn the battalion. We dispersed quickly, taking up positions at a safe distance from the track, then stalking it, gradually catching up until we recognized it as a Valentine. Still suspicious, as the enemy was said to be using British tanks in some sectors, I came alongside, covering the turret with my Bren. It was British all right, coming out for repairs. The commander told me that we had carried the first layer of the enemy's minefields. Some tanks had got through but the enemy, recovered from his initial shock, was giving the infantry a sticky time. The next lot of minefields, well covered by machine-guns and snipers, were deeper than anticipated, and the sappers were suffering many casualties.

I hastened back to HQ with this news.

A few hours later the battalion advanced. We passed the dressing station where I had received my baptism of fire, and went cautiously through the gap of the first enemy minefield, now marked and lighted by the sappers, and with a double track. The column halted at the top of a slight rise. Ahead the view was a kaleidoscope of moving lights – bursting shells, burning vehicles, sprays of tracer reaching up at unseen planes, and the blue-white, irregular lines of the fire returned by the Messerschmitts. We waited half an hour, during which there was much coming and going of senior officers and liaison officers.

We entered another minefield, which seemed to go on forever. The car began to swerve from side to side.

'What's the matter?' I asked quickly. 'Is there something wrong with the steering?'

'I just can't seem to keep awake, Sir,' said Johnston.

I took over and suddenly felt very tired. I forced myself to concentrate, acutely aware of what lay outside the verges.

Dawn came. I don't remember watching it or noticing it until I looked around and realized that we were moving slowly nose to tail in a vast minefield. There was another regiment close to us on our right 100 yards away, and beyond that another, and yet another; endless streams of armour, and the same on the left.

We halted, wondering what was going on at the head of the column. A ridge in front of us was being criss-crossed by enemy machine-gun fire, but none of our tanks climbed it. Wireless silence was now ended and word came from the leading tank that there were still fifty yards of gap to be cleared; the sappers were being mown down and couldn't work any faster. Two vehicles blew up on mines in the column to our left. Then I saw a ball of white light appear over the ridge, coming our way very slowly; then it accelerated beyond imaginable speed, passing over the car with an ear-splitting crack. There was a clank behind us and a Crusader tank appeared to have jumped to one side like a sleeping animal suddenly wakened. Its track was hanging loose and it had in fact shifted about a foot.

'Eighty-eight,' whispered Johnston, 'Christ!'

I crouched as low into the little open vehicle as I could. The 88-mm shot was an overthrow, which sounds as harmless as a cricket ball, but is actually lethal if it hits you. We could not go forward until the gap was cleared, nor could we go back because of the miles of vehicles stretched behind us like beads threaded along the narrow track. We were the perfect Aunt Sally, the anti-tank gunner's dream. But because of the courage of our infantry, who had 'waded' through the mines and attacked a number of gun positions, the enemy failed to take advantage of our plight.

A voice, shrill with panic, came over the wireless. 'For Christ's sake, we must go forward or back. If we stay here it will be a massacre!'

Authority was quick to interrupt: 'Shut up and get off the air!'

Somehow the gap was cleared and the leading tanks surged ahead and fanned out on the forward slope of the ridge. I was ordered onto the crest with a platoon of our lorried infantry. We spotted several gun positions. The infantry dealt with two of them and we engaged a third with our Brens. Over to the right was a blazing mass of British equipment. A troop of 25-pounders with their quads, and half a squadron of tanks, which had somehow got through the minefield in the dark, had been caught on the skyline by the enemy artillery at first light.

By now the greater part of our battalion was clear of the minefield. The Crusaders and Grants were on the ridge, the Shermans being kept in reserve as a surprise packet. But the secret was out, a number of them from other regiments having already been hit. Later in the day a guttural voice came up on our frequency: "'Ullo Tommy! 'Ullo Tommy! 'Ow do you like losing all your nice new tanks?'

Over the ridge was yet another minefield and beyond that a wide buff-coloured plain, across which ran a line of black cairns. We had not suspected the existence of this minefield and in our confusion got some of the wire caught up in a rear wheel. It was serious enough to require a fitter's assistance. Spotting another gun position, I sent Johnston back to find a fitter and went on foot to a Gunner OP tank. I was pointing out the target to the officer in command when there was a resounding clang and the tank shuddered. I felt heat on my shin and looked down. The shot that had struck the tank, a spent 50-mm, was lying beneath the rear sprocket. It had come close enough to tear my trouser-leg. If I'd been standing two inches nearer ... I instantaneously scrambled aboard.

By now the sun had risen. As soon as Johnston returned we took up a position of observation. Tank after tank, squadron after squadron, regiment after regiment had been pouring through the gap. Now a whole brigade was occupying an area that would normally be held by a single squadron. The infantry were dug in on the forward slope. It had developed into a slogging match so there was no scope for my troop. We sat about fifty yards forward of the tanks, and could see no more than they could. It was noisy, too, as not only were we in the line of the enemy fire, but shells from our own side screamed over and past us. At one point a round of armour-piercing fired from behind without sufficient elevation struck the ground five yards away.

As the day wore on I began to feel tired and sleepy. My head was aching from the sun and the strain of peering for long periods through binoculars. Everything seemed unreal. How could I, a peace-loving pedagogue, find myself actually in a battle, where at any moment I might become one of the anonymous, statistical dead? 'Heavy casualties were inflicted on the enemy; we lost only 200 men ... '

I looked around in numb wonder, as though I were in the eye of a hurricane, aware of everything happening around me, yet not part of it. Through my binoculars I stared at twelve small black objects. They looked like cairns until they began to grow bigger. I went on staring stupidly, thinking that cairns should not be moving, then, almost too late, realized that they were enemy tanks grinding towards us. Hastily I reported them, cursing myself for not doing so before, and hoping that no one had noticed my inefficiency.

I felt ravenously hungry, and knew that the longest day in my life must be drawing to a close at last. My watch must have stopped because it read twelve noon. I called Control on the wireless requesting signal time. Control said twelve noon and to wind my watch and not ask silly questions.

A little later Paddy, the Quartermaster, came round with rations. He nearly ran over the corpse of a British infantryman lying near my position, wearing a greatcoat, grotesque in the brilliant sunshine. My own greatcoat had fallen off the car and 'Q' had none to spare, but that night he gave me one as we went into leaguer. Despite the rather sickly smell I was glad of its protection against the cold night-time dew. Next day we took up the same positions. The corpse was still there, but now had no greatcoat.

The second day began much like the first. Beyond the minefield, some 3000 yards away, we could see the German positions. We sat on the ridge and watched and watched, our nerves battling with our fatigue. We did have some action, however, when we spotted what looked like an orders group of enemy officers within range, and sprayed them with the Bren until they dispersed.

Shelling from both sides was intense all day. In the morning fifteen enemy tanks were knocked out when they counter-attacked, and the rest withdrew.

Time dragged by until four o'clock in the afternoon. I began to doze, when I heard a click in my earphones followed by the CO's incisive voice, speaking in the familiar 'veiled language': 'Charlie Don Group,' our call-sign, 'prepare to support our friends, who are going to make a path through the cabbage patch, with covering fire and smoke if necessary. Charlie Don Group, off.' Which, being interpreted, meant that the Royal Engineers were going to clear a gap in the minefield, in a perfect illustration of their battle role, which is to enable our troops to advance, and prevent the enemy from doing so.

We were astonished. A gap, in broad daylight, in full sight of the enemy! The minefield began about fifty yards ahead and stretched back into the heat haze through a bumpy, scrubby patch of sulphur-coloured desert. We would have a grandstand view.

Soon an officer and two men appeared in front of us. The officer was carrying what looked like a hoover, his sergeant had a tommy-gun and the sapper a collection of objects that looked like chromium-plated lampshades. The officer walked forward into the minefield, sweeping his hoover from side to side. Every now and again he paused, pointing to a spot on the ground and the sapper placed one of his lampshades on it.

When they had gone about forty yards another party followed, digging up the mines indicated by the lampshades, heaping them to one side, and laying white tapes to mark the verges of the lane that had been made. We watched, fascinated, as these men carried out the most dangerous job as deliberately and coolly as though they were strolling around a shop selecting items from the shelves. We were tense, watching the gap that we were to use that night being made, and scanned the enemy lines for any sign of an attempt to interrupt the sappers' work. They were operating fast, and by now the leading group was hidden behind a small ridge.

Suddenly we heard a burst of small arms fire; then another. We saw the second group of men fling themselves down. One of them started wriggling his way back. A strange hush fell over the battlefield.

A few minutes later the rustle in my earphones ceased: a message was coming.

'Robert Able' – my troop's call-sign. I listened carefully.

'Robert Able, our friend's leader has been hit. He is lying at the extreme right edge of the cabbage patch, about 600 yards forward. Will you send one of your little chaps and see what you can do to help him? Good luck. Over.'

'Robert Able – OK. Off.'

Since speed was obviously necessary I decided to go myself, and summoned Johnston.

The little car started forward, skirting the wire as it went. I stood up and studied the minefield as we gathered speed. Every now and then we heard the whistling ping of a bullet. I could see no one at first, but there was a fold in the ground ahead which obscured some of the view. We raced into the fold and up the other side. As we topped the rise I heard Johnston, even above the sound of the engine, sharply draw in his breath. A German armoured car, an eight-wheeler, was moving slowly in our direction, its 37-mm gun pointing straight at us.

'Keep going! Swerve right!' I yelled. There was no chance of escaping to the left, for we were flanked on that side by the minefield. To stop would have been fatal. The only hope was to outmanoeuvre our swift, powerful opponent. Johnston's driving was magnificent. He veered right without losing an inch of speed, wheeled round in front of the German car and fled back, weaving from left to right, from right to left, towards our own lines.

An armour-piercing shell passed close by, followed by another, then one on the far side.

I seized the microphone. 'Robert Able – Am being chased by an eight-wheeler. Will try to lead him onto your guns. Watch out for me. Off.'

I looked over my shoulder. The gigantic vehicle was gaining on us. I called up again. 'Robert Able – Could I have smoke as soon as you see me? Over.'

'Robert Able – OK, off to you. Charlie Don Group, you heard that. Prepare to put down smoke for Robert Able. Off.'

At last our tanks came into view. We could see the tops of their turrets above the ridge, and here and there a commander standing up, binoculars to his eyes. I saw the white wake of a smoke-shell, which landed just behind us. Good shooting! The tank commander who had fired it gave the range over the wireless. At once a dozen more followed, and we could see behind us a fine bank of smoke forming, and – most blessed relief – no armoured car.

As we reached the haven of the battalion area, I said to Johnston: 'We haven't got that sapper out. If we run the car into the gap we can get near enough to do the last bit on foot. How about it?'

'OK by me, Sir! Let's take the Bren.'

I clicked a full magazine into the gun and stuffed a couple more into my pockets. We drove into the gap, then leapt out and crawled forward, feeling with our fingers for mines. Johnston, with the Bren, was a bit slower, so I waited for him behind a mound. When he reached me he pointed towards some scrub: 'Look, Sir – men!'

'What do you make of them?'

'Ities, I think. Watch out, Sir!'

He cocked the gun and fired several bursts in the direction of some men running across in front of us. I gave him another magazine. He cleared that.

'Like a shot, Sir? It's good shooting!'

'No, no. You're on the target – your bird.' He fired again.

'Now, Sir, we've no ammo left. Shall I go back and get some more?'

'Yes. Look, I think I can see the sapper lying out there. I won't be able to drag him back by myself, but I may be able to prevent his being taken prisoner. Tell the chaps when you get back to cover me – and for God's sake not to shoot me up!'

'OK, Sir.' He wriggled off.

For a moment I didn't move. I felt very alone now that Johnston had gone. I studied the ground for the best route, then, suddenly deciding to risk the mines, got up and rushed forward 150 yards. Now I was very near the sapper. One more effort, another forty yards or so, and I would make it. Just in front of me was a slit trench. I rose and flung myself into it.

Resting a few seconds in order to collect my wits and my strength, I looked over the edge through my binoculars at the body lying immobile out there.

It wasn't the sapper; it was the corpse of a New Zealander, now very decomposed. I could see the pointed Boy Scout hat, half covered in sand, lying by his head.

Well, I thought, that's that. But what's happened to the sapper?

I looked around. A movement caught my eye. Three men had disappeared behind a mound. I trained my binoculars on the place. Hullo, what the – ? It was an anti-tank gun position, magnificently camouflaged, and right on the line that our tanks were to follow that night. I swept the glasses round. There was another. I could see four in all. This information must be got back at all costs.

I had given up all hope of finding the sapper, and now that it had become imperative for me to return I wondered if I'd been spotted by the enemy. If only I could communicate with the tanks! A little smoke, and all would be well.

A bullet whistled over the trench. So I had been seen. Resolving to escape before any further attentions, I raised myself to take a last glance round, and quickly got down again. Three men were advancing towards me, armed with sub-machine-guns. When I looked again they had disappeared. Now was the time to get away! I half rose. They were there again, not more than fifty yards away. I took out my Smith and Wesson revolver, wishing it were a Luger or a tommy-gun. It wasn't likely that I could score a hit at that range, but perhaps I could keep them down while I scrambled over the parapet of the trench. The men were still coming on.

I raised the revolver and, keeping it well elevated, fired three shots, which must have come close, as they dropped instantly.

Suddenly the blast of an explosion knocked me down. I flattened myself on the bottom of the trench. A mortar shell had landed not ten yards away. I *must* get away now, before one of those things fell on top of me. I jumped out and ran back in the direction of the battalion. There was a scream of bullets. I flung myself down, expecting to be blown to bits by a mine, and waited. Another sprint, another scream of bullets. By now my lungs were bursting and red-hot, and I was drenched with sweat and trembling with exhaustion. Each time I ran a shorter distance, staying longer on the ground. The bullets shrieked over me even when I was prone. I tried to dig myself in with my fingers, to flatten myself into the sand, urged on by the powerful, futile instinct that possesses a hunted man as his pursuers close in.

Gradually, lying there exhausted, I became aware of a difference in the sound of the bullets. As my breathing eased I listened more carefully. It was a familiar sound, the deliberate, menacing rat-tat-tat-tat of the Besa machine-gun. So our tanks were covering me. It was worth making a final dash for it now. I got up and ran, ran as I had never run before, till I found myself among a little group of British infantrymen and sappers lying at the edge of the gap, where all work had ceased. One of the sappers, a sergeant, was wounded in the arm.

An infantryman came up to me.

'You OK, Sir? Bags of enemy out there!'

'Yes, I'm OK. They've got anti-tank guns too – '

'Nice run you did, Sir! I nearly fired at you, then I saw 'ow fast you was running so I knew it must be an Itie or one of our chaps – '

'Thanks,' I said, 'I decided to forget the mines.'

'It's a dummy field, Sir,' said the sapper Sergeant, '90 per cent duds.'

'Thank God for that. Well, I'm packing it in, Sergeant. You'd better come along too and have that arm dressed.'

'It's nothing, Sir. I'll stay and see the fun.'

'Sergeant, you'll come with me. That's an order.'

We crawled off and in a moment were joined by a third figure crawling along beside us, helping the Sergeant.

'Hullo, Johnston! What have you been doing?'

'Having a shoot, Sir. We'll need to see the "Q" tonight for some more ammo.'

'What! Have you used it all? Did you hit any of them?'

'One or two, Sir, I think.'

'He fair mowed 'em dahn, Sir,' said the Sergeant, and fainted.

We were now almost within the battalion area, so I left the Sergeant with Johnston and went on alone. When help was sent out to them I reported to Pete's tank.

'Enjoyed yourself?' he enquired laconically.

'Well, Sir, it wasn't altogether a wild-goose chase – '

'There's your wild goose,' he interrupted, grinning and stabbing his finger towards a captain in the Royal Engineers who was being attended to by our MO, the imperturbable Scotsman Macmillan. 'Wounded in the foot – crawled out of the field under cover of the smoke we put down for you, and was nearly run over by your eight-wheeler friend before he departed in a panic. He tells me there are anti-tank guns in the "field".'

'Yes, Sir, four. Fifty-millimetre.'

'Good. Well, go over to the Gunner OP officer and if you can spot them from there, help him to blast them.'

I walked towards the OP tank. As I passed Mac's ambulance I could see the pale, pinched face of the sapper officer as he was lifted in on a stretcher. I smiled at him; he raised his arm and waved, the quick greeting and farewell of two people who had been unwitting partners for a few hours in a lethal game.

I mounted the gunner's tank and explained my mission. Soon the air was tortured with the sound of a dozen shells shrieking in train and exploding, four at a time, throwing up great jets of sand like dirty candle-flames. This was repeated three times, once on each enemy gun position. Then, during the silence that followed the final explosion, we swept the area through our binoculars. Not a movement was to be seen.

That night we were to go through the minefield in front of us. We lined up as before, only this time we were not the leading regiment. Everything went well until the infantry of the regimental group we were following went in. Then all hell broke loose. The enemy had two 88s trained on the gap, firing in enfilade. They hit a petrol wagon. Now the bombers came over. They were deadly accurate: soon twenty vehicles were blazing. The heat was so intense you could not go nearer than thirty yards. The whole brigade fired at the planes, a huge pyramid of ascending red lights converging and fading at the apex. The gap was blocked so we withdrew and went into leaguer. One of my cars had been hit and smashed, but the crew were unharmed.

As we approached our area Bob ordered me to lead his tank by a few yards.

'Are there any mines about?' I asked.

'Don't know,' he replied, 'that's why I want you in front of me!'

Peering back through the swirling dust I could just see the satanic grin on his face.

At 3 a.m. we were ordered to try again. This time we got through, past the stinking, smouldering vehicles, and fanned out into the plain beyond. Suddenly, simultaneously, about 300 yards ahead, four tanks 'brewed up'. A spurt of flame in the air, a detonation, then the rattling and racket of the ammunition exploding. In a few minutes they were glowing like gold in the morning sunlight. Two more, then another – in five minutes there were twelve. Sometimes we saw – or thought we saw – frantic figures moving jerkily into the shadows from the flashing blaze and then, suicidally, running back again. It was an unreal scene, like a fantastic silent film accompanied by the terrible music of battle.

Our second attempt to pierce the enemy anti-tank gun screen by night had failed. He simply waited for us and opened up at point-blank range. The leading regiment lost more than a complete squadron. We were ordered to withdraw. Ignominiously, with the dawn coldly revealing us to the enemy, we turned about and, forming a column, marched back through the gap to take up our old positions for yet another day. For a long time we remembered this as 'the night of the brew-up'.

The enemy artillery now had the range of our position on the ridge, and the continuous bombardment strained our nerves, Johnston's even more than mine. At first this puzzled me, since he was one of the coolest customers I had ever met but, as he fidgeted about beside me, I realized why. Essentially he was a man of action. Armed and in among the enemy he was quite happy, and in normal circumstances he was restless-ly busy, but now, crouching in the car, he had nothing to do.

'Wot good are we doing 'ere anyway, Sir?' he asked peevishly.

I explained that if we passed even one valuable piece of information during the day we would contribute materially to the success of the battle.

He snorted. 'Wot can we see from 'ere that the others can't see, eh?'

'Shut up!' I exploded, 'Control yourself!'

His mood echoed mine too exactly for comfort.

That day I lost another car, Bert's, on a mine, and the commander, one of my best, was killed. Corporal Bennett, who had been guiding this car on foot through a mine 'swamp', was badly wounded.

The mind moves strangely in a long static battle like this. One began to understand the unbelievable stress which in the First World War often resulted in shell-shock, in our war called being 'bomb-happy'. After a few weeks' rest many people got over it, but not so Andy C., one of our officers in another squadron. He jumped out of his tank and ran away during the first night of the battle. A man of exceptional charm, with whom I became very friendly at base depot while we waited for our postings, he was a natural leader, with a bubbling sense of humour. It was inconceivable that he should lose his nerve so soon, and yet perhaps this was due to his innate honesty. Many of us fought on because we were afraid to show that we were afraid, so Andy's surrender might be seen as inverted courage. I used to wonder what became of him. At least the barbarity of being shot for cowardice was not applied in this war.

The shock of my first few days in battle was so severe that almost consciously I built around myself a protective shelter within which my mind ricocheted between past and future, as though deliberately avoiding the hideousness of the present.

Happenings around me assumed an extra significance. Whenever I saw a man killed or wounded I did not see him as such –
I saw his mother in some suburban terrace chatting with her
neighbour over the garden fence, ignorant of how her life was
being savaged at this very moment in the desert.

Then I found that I'd been staring at my hands for some
time, thinking how well they had served me all my life, and
how I had taken them for granted, noting the play of muscles
when I moved my fingers. Then I thought, 'Christ, this is
awful! Is this bomb-happiness?' I glanced at Johnston to see if
he had noticed me, but he was concentrating on opening a tin
of bully without showing himself above the side of the car. I
experienced again the sensation of plunging my hands into
cool water, of grasping a tennis racket, holding a knife and
fork, tying a knot in a piece of string, clinging onto the wet
sheet of my dinghy in a choppy sea, running my fingers
through a girl's hair. How much one owes to one's hands; how
ghastly it would be if they were mangled, rendered useless for
life. I became melodramatic and wondered if this line of
thought were prophetic.

A shell landed ten yards in front of us, burrowing deep
before bursting. The blast must have been almost vertical for it
hardly touched us, but hot fragments came showering down
for several seconds afterwards.

'So near!' I thought. 'How lucky we hadn't halted there! If I
moved the car a little over to the right a shell might land just
where we are and we'd have another hair-breadth escape. On
the other hand, it might land on the spot we moved to. Better
to stay here. Or is it?' An agony of futile ifs and ans pursued
each other round and round my mind. 'If I go … if I stay … if I
look up now a bullet will get me … if I keep down and wait,
then it will get me when I do look up … better to look up now.
Or is it? Oh Christ!'

Bob, so sensitive to the feelings of those under his command,
appeared beside us, having strolled over from his tank as
though enjoying a quiet walk in the garden after dinner, and
just as casually asked us how we were.

'Bad luck losing those two cars, but it wasn't your fault.'

He shaded his eyes and peered across the sand towards a
small area which was being 'stonked' by one of our guns.

'What's that fool firing at – can you see?'

'I can see his target – that black spot by the left-hand cairn – but I can't make out what it is.'

'Looks like a gun to me. He's a bloody idiot, wasting AP on it. Anyway, that's not what I came over for. Take your car back as far as you can, and have a meal. I'll expect you back in an hour.'

Johnston grinned and slipped into gear before I had time to give him the order. We felt like schoolboys given an unexpected half-holiday on a fine afternoon. Back through the minefield we raced, as far as the echelon. The enemy began shelling this area so we turned back and found a comparatively quiet place 300 yards behind RHQ. Fifteen minutes of our precious hour wasted. We made an enormous brew of tea and heated a tin of M and V (meat and veg – a desert delicacy). In my excitement I poured half a bag of salt into the tea, thinking it was sugar. Johnston said nothing, but his look was sufficient. Another ten minutes wasted and two pints of precious water. Then for a few minutes we rested in silence, too tired for talking.

On the way back past RHQ I stopped to receive my instructions from Pete.

'I want you to contact the armour with the New Zealanders, which is operating due north of us. We are going through the minefield at 2300 hours tonight, will leaguer on the other side and be in battle positions at first light. Find out what they are doing and arrange recognition signals. Your Squadron Leader has assumed direct command of your troop.'

It seemed an easy enough mission, the first thing to discover being the location of NZ HQ. Our own Brigade HQ told me that the New Zealanders were two miles due north, but not to try the direct route as it was getting dark and the minefields were not yet cleared. There were two options: to go right back to the Qattara Road and follow the NZ axis forward, or to follow the ridge which the Eighth Army was holding until I came to the tanks (9th Armoured Brigade). The first would have been easier but would have taken too long, so I decided to follow the ridge.

We moved on in the growing dark, listening all the time to the traffic on the battalion net. It sounded as though the third attempt to pass through the gap had started. I heard a tank commander say, 'Hit by AP. Gunner killed. Withdrawing.' And Bob replying, 'Bad luck, but you must expect casualties in battle. Do not withdraw. We'll get you another gunner.'

A shell landed 200 yards ahead. A jagged splinter whirred between us and buried itself in the wireless. Now we were incommunicado, cut off from the unit among strangers, trying to find other strangers in the dark. We ran into several slit trenches and were deservedly cursed by the infantry cowering in them.

When at length we were really lost we halted to find our bearings. I dismounted and walked on a few paces. Turning back towards the car my eye was caught by a large circular object resting against one of the front wheels. Thinking it was a stone I was about to kick it aside when I realized it was a mine. Marvelling at our escape I stood still, holding my breath. I heard voices to our right and to my relief discovered an infantry Battalion HQ.

'New Zealanders?' they said. 'Oh yes, they were here this afternoon but they've gone now, God knows where. Don't you go swanning about in the dark – you'll hit a mine for a cert.'

'Are there any tank units around here?'

'No, they've all gone.'

That knocked the point off my mission. I decided to go back the way I had come. It was important that Pete should know he would have no contact with the armour on his right.

Everything looked different in the dark. Slowly, making many errors, we retraced our path. We came at last to the lighted gap through which the battalion had gone. I was half-way through when I realized how stupid I was being: I had no idea where the leaguer would be. We turned about. The enemy was taking pot-luck with his 88s and firing at random over our lines. Occasionally a flare would be dropped from a plane, illuminating the whole area.

We came on a tank leaguer of the famous Warwickshire Yeomanry, the only regiment to penetrate the gap at our second attempt. They had spent twenty-four hours behind enemy lines fighting hard. The CO told me our battalion had been withdrawn to five miles back, and to stay in their leaguer till the morning.

It was a noisy night. 88s were criss-crossing the leaguer but, because of the ridge between us and them, were unable to depress sufficiently. Several wireless masts were carried away but no other damage was done.

The following day I asked the brigadier commanding a neighbouring brigade if he knew where our battalion was. He didn't, but took me to his brigade-major to find out.

On the way he told me that the enemy were expected to counter-attack heavily that day, and our disastrous attempt to break through two nights earlier had cost him the best part of a regiment. The brigade-major showed me on the map where our Brigade HQ was heading for. They were moving in when I arrived, so I had to wait for nearly an hour before a harassed G3 told me what I wanted to know.

His directions were clear and the route not difficult to follow. I had to make my way to the Qattara Road, proceed south until I came to the 'Bottle Track', turn left and continue for 1000 yards. Things did not look promising as I went along the 'Bottle Track'. I could see no tanks at all, nothing but a series of encampments of Pioneers and dumps of equipment. I stopped when my speedometer showed 1000 yards, to find myself surrounded by a platoon of Basuto Pioneers. They seemed happy to see me, if the wide grins on their faces were anything to go by.

'Any tanks about here?' I asked. At once twenty voices expressed their individual views at the same time.

I held up my hand for silence and said, very clearly, trying to get a strong note of query into my voice: 'Tanks?'

Twenty enthusiastic hands pointed simultaneously in twenty different directions. One man wore sergeant's stripes. I spoke to him.

'Sergeant!'

'Yais, Sah!'

'Have you seen any tanks around here?'

'Yais, Sah!'

'Where?'

'Yais, Sah!' His grinning face, so friendly, so conscious of having helped, beguiled me from my frustration.

'Where are your OFFICERS?' At last communication was established. A man was despatched and returned with a British captain.

'There's a regiment of tanks over behind that ridge,' he said. 'You can go straight – no mines.'

We thanked him and set off. It was now past midday. We found the battalion dispersed there, most of them cooking and washing.

One of the first people I saw was Bob, surrounded by a group of his officers and NCOs. He frowned slightly as I saluted; then the quick half-smile that always prefaced some friendly jibe: 'You've no right to come back – I've just posted you as missing!'

We rested all that day. 'Resting' in an armoured regiment means maintenance on the vehicles, cleaning the guns, rearranging your maps, washing and mending your clothes – perhaps leaving time to wash, write letters, cook and eat meals.

That evening a mobile canteen came our way and we bought two dozen bottles of beer, which we buried in the sand up to the necks, in the hope of cooling them down. Later we had a meal and afterwards, seated in a circle on empty petrol-cans, got down to the serious business of beer-drinking. Everyone had some story to tell of the battle. Everyone was aware of the missing faces. Soon, however, the sense of camaraderie asserted itself and I knew I was privileged to have under my command a team of rare quality.

'Funny thing, Sir,' said Lance-Corporal Beck, 'we didn't like the CO when he took over – teaching us all that stuff in the delta as if we'd never been in action before. But now he's quite different – knows his stuff all right, and he don't badger you on the air, and he tells you if you've done well. He's OK.'

'I know,' I answered, 'but if we hadn't had all that training then, we wouldn't be where we are now.'

'And a bloody good thing too! Cor! Think of going down the street now – half an hour to closing-time, and the missus waiting up for you with a broom-'andle!'

Several times the enemy planes came over, fast, weaving to and fro, dropping their bombs and scurrying away again. They couldn't help hitting something in this concentration of vehicles. Fortunately for us the ack-ack was intense and continuous, forcing the raiders to spend not a second longer than necessary over our lines.

We turned in early. At 3 a.m. there was a 'flap' move. Discipline was good and although this was entirely unexpected we were in our vehicles, loaded up and ready to move in twenty minutes. The brigade was moving north towards the sea and by first light we had taken up battle positions on the long Miteriyah Ridge, where our infantry were already dug in.

From here you could see the enemy plainly, scarcely 1000 yards away. We were given a cold welcome by our infantry, who said we attracted shell-fire, which indeed we did. But their chief worry was snipers. One infantry battalion lost thirty officers and men, including their CO, during the morning. There was little for my depleted troop to do, as nearly all the cars I had lost were patrol commanders' vehicles, those fitted with a wireless. My own damaged wireless had been repaired, so I was included in the regimental net. Our proper role of observation now denied to us, we spent the time ferrying wounded back to the regimental aid posts.

An excited voice came up on the air from one of the tanks: 'I think I've spotted the sniper! He's in that derelict tank right in front of me!'

'Can you get him?' asked Bob.

'If I go over the ridge – not from here.'

'Do what you think best.'

I saw the Crusader dip over the ridge and disappear. I heard the commander's running commentary. 'Yes, he is in the tank – I can get him now. Am being fired on.'

Then, a few seconds later, 'This is getting hot. Can you put down smoke?'

'You're too far. Get back as quickly as you can. Are you OK?'

No answer. Another voice: 'He's been brewed up. The crew's baling out – they look in a bad way.'

A spiral of black smoke was rising from that direction.

'Is there any way of helping those chaps?'

'No – unless the chickens can do something.'

'Chickens' was the battalion code-name for my troop of little cars.

'OK,' I said, 'I'm on my way.'

Before I had put the mike down Johnston had let in the clutch. He was smiling. I wondered if he remembered the similar mission a few days earlier, when we had been chased by the eight-wheeled armoured car. The past disappeared in the reality of the present as we careered down the forward slope of the ridge. A spatter of machine-gun bullets ricocheted off the side of the vehicle. The tank had gone much further than I'd thought, but there was no drawing back now. I asked for smoke.

'Sorry,' the reply came, 'you're out of range.'

We ran in beside the burning tank, which was broadside on to the enemy and so formed a shield for us, and dismounted. Three of the crew were lying some way out in the open, apparently unable to move. At this moment my attention became riveted on a white and mauve cigarette packet a yard or two away which contrasted vividly with the sand. Its very irrelevance fascinated me.

Johnston glanced into the turret.

'No one alive in there.'

I looked at the men lying out in the open and hesitated. Little spurts of sand were being kicked up between me and them, and I realized distantly that we were under heavy and accurate machine-gun fire. The cigarette packet seemed to be staring back at me, like an accusation. I raised my head and saw the expression in one of the men's eyes, helpless, like that of a hurt animal. He was putting his trust in me to perform some sort of miracle, and I was failing him.

As though moved by an external will or impulse I ran out and dragged him back into the shade of the tank. His leg had been shot away below the knee and the bare, splintered shinbone was sticking out. Johnston collected one of the others, and this sudden activity seemed to bring life to the third, for he got back into the lee of the tank under his own steam. I picked up the man Johnston had rescued and tried to make him comfortable. He had lost his arm and most of his shoulder, and I remember thinking, as my hand sank into the warm, raw flesh, how strange it was that I should be able to do this when normally the sight of a little blood made me feel sick.

On the return journey the car stopped 100 yards from the crest. Johnston, his face working in desperation, said, 'We've been hit, Sir!'

We off-loaded the men and Johnston went on foot to get

help. I lit cigarettes and handed them round. For the first time one of the men spoke: 'Christ!', the awful awareness dawning on him, 'Christ! I've lost my leg!'

Another tank came out to us, a Crusader, and we put the wounded men onto the platform behind the turret. Johnston stayed with them and I clung to the tow-rope. The tank reversed. An armour-piercing shell passed us about six yards away, dragging the loose sand up in the vacuum behind it, like a fantastically fast speedboat in a smooth sea. Then another went by, this time closer, and I knew that the third time he would not miss. The possibilities flashed across my mind: if it hit the back the petrol-tanks would explode; if it hit the turret it would kill the commander, operator and gunner and, if it penetrated right through, would take my head with it; if it hit the front it would kill the driver.

It hit the back. There was a tremendous reverberation and a white pillar of flame. Somehow the wounded men got down onto the sand. Then came the most terrible sound I have ever heard: a frenzied, agonized screaming, which seemed to have a hint of mad laughter in it. It was Johnston. His clothes were blazing from head to foot. Not only his clothing, his flesh as well. We threw him onto the ground and tried to tear his shirt and slacks off. He pushed his trousers down to his ankles, where they caught on his boots. The irons were white-hot. The pain in my hands was excruciating and I knew I was reaching a point when I could stand it no more, but kept telling myself that there was no such point, for Johnston was suffering far beyond it, and was still alive. Still alive – he seemed to have passed beyond feeling pain and was directing us in a far-away, tired, resigned voice.

We hoisted him onto a blanket which somebody had collected and carried him back. Mac, the MO, set about tending the wounded men.

While this was going on Bob came over. He said nothing, but put his hand on my shoulder. It was almost more than I could bear. It signified the end of the action, that strange unforeseeable moment when the walls of control collapse. I looked at the wounded men, at Johnston, and understood for the first time what it meant. Up to this there had been no time to think. Now my thoughts and feelings hit me like a tidal wave. My hands suddenly started hurting like hell.

When all four wounded were in the ambulance Mac treated my hands. He bundled me in after them, fixing a card to my shirt: 'Slight burns and shock.' I protested, because I felt no shock, but Mac was adamant.

One of the men was crying, helplessly, like a small child.

'It's OK now,' I said, 'you'll be OK soon.'

'It's the relief, Sir,' he answered, 'it's such a relief ... '

We were all suffering from intense thirst. The driver gave us water in a mug. I handed it round, offering it to Johnston first.

He didn't need it.

FIVE

Hospital

Deeply sedated, I was further numbed by the rhythm of the wheels clicking along the lines, like the opening bars of Beethoven's Fifth Symphony. Did-did-de-daa, did-did-de-daa. Morse code for V. V for Victory. The Destiny Symphony. Whose destiny? Johnston is dead, Johnston is dead.

The drug was compressing my brain. Time telescoped.

All my fellow passengers were wounded, some lying on stretchers on the floor, some in bunks. For many this was a mobile ward, for others a mobile mortuary.

Hours later an ambulance to the hospital, somewhere outside Cairo. My hands soothed in a current of brine. Peace, temporary safety, cleanliness, gentleness, passive bliss.

Then the shock reminder that the army is no respecter of persons, not even wounded ones. The Ward Sister bustles in and removes the dressings from our wounds.

'What's this in aid of, Sister?' I whimper.

'Inspection by Chief Medical Officer. He likes to see the wounds, and we remove the dressings so that he won't be – '

'That's cruelty, Sister!'

' – kept waiting. Now be quiet.' She bustles out.

The pain brings tears to my eyes. The hours pass, two long hours. Footsteps beyond the open door. Mumble of approaching voices. A phrase filters through: 'The men seem comfortable ... ' A glimpse of grey-haired Brass. At last! But the footsteps fade. Another hour, and Sister comes to put our dressings on again. The CMO hadn't time to visit every ward, she says, only those for the severely wounded.

Fretful memories. All my kit is lost, including my cigarettes. How cold it was at night in the desert. Until the sun came up I wore battledress – not very hygienic, and yet, although we had so little water to wash with, we kept surprisingly clean. Sand is quite a cleaning substance, like Vim. And then that marvellous shower of rain, the first for months. Great luscious drops came slopping down; we sat outside our vehicles to enjoy it. The drops fell on the sand with a thick thumping noise, then soaked in and were lost.

A fortnight later I still had two fingers on each hand bandaged, leaving me helpless in a few minor ways. I was not supposed to get the bandages wet, so I was washed daily by an ill-tempered and ill-favoured Palestinian ATS girl. I think she was really an enemy agent, to judge by the pleasure she took in forcing the soap into my eyes. Very painful. Her name was Lottie, which suited her shrill, scolding, shrewish voice: heard in the early morning it almost made me long for the comparative peace of the battlefield.

In the NAAFI I met a charming old doctor with a long row of ribbons, who had been in every war since the Boer War. I thought I'd recovered from my so-called shock. By a coincidence shock was his special study and he told me that it is usually incurred when one is in a tight corner and too busy to be frightened. Afterwards a reaction sets in, and that is shock. If you bottle it up it can affect you for years. He described battle as having the effect of a motor smash lasting several days. This was true in my case, except that I wasn't frightened so much as horrified by what happened to my men during those last few moments at Alamein.

I remember very clearly the date of 15 November 1942, when I wrote home to describe an event that made me feel very close to my family, despite the thousands of miles between us. Listening to the wireless news after lunch, I heard the broadcast of the church bells being rung for the first time since the war began, in honour of our victory. First Westminster Abbey, then St Cuthbert's, Edinburgh, Armagh in Northern Ireland, and finally Llandaff Cathedral, near Whitchurch, where my parents lived. It had been shattered by bombs and the bells couldn't be rung because the steeple had been too badly damaged; instead, they were chimed. When the last notes had died, the announcer spoke of the 'glorious battle' in the desert. The result was glorious, but the actual battle wasn't. Like all battles it was hideous.

A few weeks later, convalescence. Sometimes I hired a minute dinghy on Lake Timsah, by Ismailia, and enjoyed the exhilaration of dodging the big craft or almost running aground in the tricky channels. In the centre of the lake King Farouk's impressive yacht was moored, its anchors embedded in concrete for fear he might use it to go abroad and stir up trouble.

In the evening a stillness wrapped the lake. The sun would slink down behind the trees as the dinghy drifted slowly through the shadows and the glassy water. The phosphorescence of tiny fish made erratic blue patterns beneath the surface, and all eternity seemed concentrated in the magic of those little moving lights.

One day I was sitting in the shade on the lawn outside the low, bleak buildings of the temporary hospital talking to a young medical officer newly arrived from England. Every time I lit a cigarette he glanced towards me, and pursed his lips.

'All right, I know, doctor. Smoking is bad for you!'

'It's not that – '

'But life is short – '

'It's not that – '

'Wait till *you've* been up in the desert for a bit – '

'Look here – '

' – you'll find you need a fag yourself sometimes.'

'Look, I'm a psychiatrist. I've noticed you always strike the match *away* from you – '

'That's because – '

'Striking the match *away* from you is a feminine trait. Do you – '

'Do I what?'

'Do you have any – '

'No.'

'You may think so but I can assure you that deep in your subconscious – '

'Do you know why I do it?'

'Yes, it's because – '

'Egyptian matches are brittle. If you strike them towards you you'll set your uniform on fire.'

'Er – '

Soon I was posted to RAC base depot for a week's sick leave. My room was the one I had occupied when I first arrived in

Egypt, and the same suffragi fussed over me like a solicitous hen. His first concern was my uniform, which he took away to be cleaned and pressed. He was particularly shocked that a lost button had been replaced by what he called a 'stafe pin': 'Not good for officer.'

I was filled with a desire to surrender to my senses, to release my mind from the bruising and numbness. I don't know which I really sought, excitement or peace. These two forces were pulling me apart. The philosophy of the soldier on active service – 'If it has your name on it, it will get you' – appealed to both. Soon I would be in battle again. Time might be short, and there was so much to do and see and feel, so much to think about and savour.

Before Alamein, when I was working at BTE HQ, I had occasionally enjoyed the company of a girl in the South African Women's Corps. She was dark-haired, with ivory skin, and somewhat statuesque, with a serenity which made me feel at peace both with her and with myself, and a beauty which made me marvel that she could tolerate, even seem to relish, the attentions of an earthy ape like me. Like Cordelia's, her voice was ever soft, gentle and low. She loved poetry and dancing and music and fun. To be with her, I believed, would give me the power I needed to put myself together again.

So one night, resplendent in my newly pressed uniform, I took her out in a taxi to Giza. We dined at Mena House, and watched King Farouk cavorting with his ladies on the dance-floor, whilst obsequious courtiers applauded their pleasure-loving monarch. Exile was not far away.

After dinner we walked across the sand to the pyramids. No moon was shining, but the night was luminous from those enormous brash Egyptian stars. We left the track and wandered under the shelving mass of Chefren's Pyramid, until we came to the ruins of the little funerary temple.

We sat down and listened to the silence. It seemed unnecessary to talk. A feeling of oneness pervaded my being, oneness with the sky, the velvet universe, the pyramid itself, the stone on which we sat. In the smell of the sand I sensed all life enclosed within me, back beyond the ancient world of Egypt to the beginning of time; to Greece and Rome, to today with the world in torment, to tomorrow, and on to eternity. And at the centre of this ageless silence, Margaret and me, at one, like the universe.

We didn't speak, even when I found her hand in mine. I didn't know when she'd put it there; nor indeed whether it was I who had enclosed hers. At last we stood up. It would be wrong to say that I kissed her; rather we kissed each other, chastely, on the lips. It was an everlasting moment, perfect in its integrity.

But next day bathos lurked. In Cairo there were two tea-shops of international repute, both known as Groppi's. One was patronized mostly by British officers and their escorts, the other by Egyptians. The one I knew, Big Groppi's, served rich and exquisite confectionery in a high glass-domed hall furnished with blood-red carpets and blood-red upholstered chairs. Potted palms of considerable majesty completed the profusion of exotic tastelessness. On this, the day before my leave ended, I took Margaret out to tea. As we got into the taxi I said casually in my best man-about-town voice, 'Groppi's, please.'

The driver waited until we were seated. Then, turning round and eyeing us with a hideous and suggestive leer, he asked, 'Beeg Gropey – or leetle Gropey?'

Not aware of the distinction I hazarded, 'Big Groppi, of course.' A trembling beside me made me look at Margaret. Why should my punctured pride move her to tears, I wondered with a certain smugness. Her handkerchief covered her face. Protectively I laid my arm round her shoulders. Pride was even further punctured when I realized that she was laughing all the way to Groppi's.

Back to the Desert

Next day I joined a convoy going up the coast road. In winter the desert has a different character. Instead of the interminable sand, there is a sort of coarse grass sprouting here and there, sparse and hardy, creating little dark patches on the landscape. In that moment of semi-darkness when the sun sank behind the horizon, the view induced nostalgic memories of an Irish bog.

For some days we bumped along in a lorry until we reached a rest camp by the shore. Despite the coldness of the mid-December days we bathed in water that was still warm.

My main memory of this trip is of one of the drivers who had a fine tenor voice and a comprehensive repertoire. At night when we halted we would be moved by the despair of *Pagliacci*, or stirred by Elgar's 'Land of Hope and Glory'. His forte, however, was a ditty that lodged permanently (and irritatingly) in my mind. This was a parody, sung with all the glutinous sentimentality of its original, the German lullaby adopted from the Afrika Corps by the Eighth Army, 'Lili Marlene'. His version was entitled 'On Missing the Boat Home':

> Didn't use me ointment, didn't use me loaf,
> Didn't use me nettin', I bin a stupid oaf:
> Oh what a silly ass I bin,
> I didn't take me mepacrine;
> Now I've got malaria, malaria's got me down.

We moved on, and in a few days came to Divisional HQ, where I made enquiries about the location of my battalion. When he heard my name a staff officer called me over and handed me a note. I found it hard to understand, because the message, signed by General Harding, the Divisional Commander, was so unexpected and so overwhelming.

That evening I wrote home: 'For some mysterious reason I have been awarded a decoration. Can't think why. I'm happy about it for one reason – it was for helping to save lives, not to take them.'

I found the battalion resting near Merduma, after their magnificent action at El Agheila, where they had knocked out seven M13 tanks of the Italian Centauro Armoured Division.

The land here was flat, with clusters of palm trees giving shade. Everyone was in triumphant mood and I received a welcome that made me glad to be a member of such a close, if enormous, family. All the fears and tribulations of the past few weeks evaporated, replaced by a serene feeling of being home again.

Pete met me at the door of his tent with a big grin and a handshake. As ever, he was immaculately turned out, making no concessions to the casual informality adopted by most officers in the desert. His Napoleonic strut was even more pronounced, and on his chest was the ribbon of the DSO, awarded in recognition of his masterly leadership at Alam Halfa.

He tapped my ribbon. 'Splendid, splendid! A great credit to the battalion!' For a moment I had a vision of my housemaster after I'd contributed a goal towards another cup for the dining-hall mantelpiece.

'Now, Peter, your future.'

'Yes, Sir. I suppose I'll take over my troop again. I hear Henry commanded while I was away.'

'Yes indeed. He's done very well with them. Splendid fellow. Splendid. Now you, you've had a tough time. Bit out of touch. Getting back into battle after a wound is worse than your first battle. Have to build up your nerve again, y'know.'

'Sir, I'm sure my nerve's OK. I'm looking forward to – '

'Yes yes I know, I wouldn't expect anything different. But you've proved yourself in battle. We've got to look ahead.'

'But Sir – '

'Exactly. Yes, you're quite right. Your future career. To start with I think you should see how things are worked at Brigade, so – '

'But Sir – '

' – so I've arranged for you to go there for a couple of months as liaison officer.'

'But – '

'You never know what it will lead to. A staff job, for instance.'

'But – '

'Good. I knew you'd be grateful. You've a great future in the army. Transport's laid on. You start tomorrow. That's all. Good luck!'

Dazed and disappointed I shuffled ankle-deep in loose sand towards the mess tent. As a fighting soldier the last thing I wanted was to be on the staff. While recognizing their necessity I professed to distrust and despise all staff wallahs.

My squadron leader was sympathetic, but ironically practical.

'Well, we've done without you since Alamein. Another month or two won't make much difference. And at brigade, you know, you can do a lot for us on the QT.'

Staff Officer

Brigade was leaguered on high ground a few miles inland. The surface here was hard, made up of layers of stone that seemed welded by some ancient conflagration, level overall but wrinkled, a grey-brown moonscape, utterly inhospitable and lonely.

There were many specialist officers here: doctors, chaplains, gunners, sappers and others, all highly trained and highly efficient. Most were public school and Oxbridge, ineffably self-confident, laconic in conversation, formal in manner. I was treated civilly but never felt at ease, never shook off the status of new boy.

Life was very different from that in a tank battalion. Instead of my accustomed place in a hard-skinned tank or armoured car I found myself in a jeep, horribly unprotected, armed only with a revolver, a wretched toy compared with the great guns in the tanks. An HQ is a mobile administrative unit, its offices in dozens of vehicles, each designed for its own specific purpose. We were static now, preparing the next phase, the long advance towards Tripoli.

In the evenings we relaxed in a tent that served as the officers' mess. After supper we played cards for money, usually pontoon, but there was a strict rule that no one might lose more than a few pence in an evening. During my first session, as I sat lonely, listening to the flat aristocratic tones around me, I was suddenly startled and delighted to hear someone speaking with a strong West of Ireland accent. It was the Roman Catholic chaplain, whom I shall call Father Joyce, a large, merry man, who loved his game of cards. Soon, however, I saw that he hated losing, so much so that he actually used to cheat. How contemptible, I thought. How could a grown man with his Christian upbringing stoop to this?

His weakness was apparent to the other officers, who of course had known him much longer. They found it rather amusing, and were extremely tolerant in their English way.

'Well,' they'd drawl, 'it's not really important. He gets a great kick out of thinking he's fooling us.' And then, what really infuriated me, they'd add with a knowing smile, 'You see, he's Irish!'

One day about noon, when the sun was at its hottest and brightest, we saw enemy planes approaching, little black dots growing relentlessly bigger, about fifteen of them in perfect formation. These were the fearsome Stukas, dive-bombers with wires attached to their wings, causing a terrifying whistling noise as they dived towards their target. We watched them swing round in a great semicircle until they were invisible between us and the sun.

At once our anti-aircraft crews raced to their guns. The rest of us could do nothing, except lie flat on the ground and hope we would not be hit. The first wave of planes screamed down. We heard our ack-ack guns firing like huge machine-guns. Even before the bombs landed the planes levelled off and soared up and away. For a moment there was silence. Then an ammunition lorry exploded and burst into flame – and another. One of our anti-aircraft guns had been hit; we could hear the screaming.

Suddenly, as another wave of bombers manoeuvred into the sun, a staff car moved out towards the stricken gun crew.

'Get back, you idiot!' someone shouted.

The car lurched and stopped, a jagged hole torn in its side. Out of it stepped a man, very deliberately, as though nothing extraordinary were happening. It was Father Joyce, the sleeves of his white shirt rolled above his elbows. He walked purposefully towards the wounded men. Bombs were bursting all around him, and bullets splintering the shale. But on he went. He bound up wounds; he gave spiritual comfort where he could not otherwise help. He never faltered, never even ducked when the bombs landed near him.

Later on I saw him, armed with a spade and a pick, digging graves through that ungiving surface.

That evening he arrived late for the game of cards, because he was writing letters to the relatives of the dead and wounded.

Bravery in battle is sometimes a matter of impulse caused by fear, an adrenalin-driven act to hide a greater fear, a fear of death through inaction, or even the fear of being thought afraid.

But Father Joyce's actions were not a matter of impulse. They were deliberate, they were continuous, aimed at helping men in mortal danger. There were no heroics for Father Joyce, no 'going over the top', rifle in hand, inspired by the thrill of combat. Had there been no war, and had I known him only in peace-time, I would probably have written him off as a petty buffoon. How many acts of courage and devotion are curtained off behind apparently uneventful lives?

Which was the real Father Joyce – the man who cheated at cards to win a few pence, or the man who risked his life so fearlessly to help those soldiers? It is an imponderable question, since it suggests that the complexity of human motives and feelings can be expressed in terms of black and white. I know that Father Joyce didn't cheat for the money, which could mean nothing to him. It may have been an act, a 'playing Irish' to amuse his fellow officers, or even a fling of contempt and defiance at their assumption of superiority. I have come to believe that his heroism was always there, always a part of him. In war it was evinced in spectacular manner, in peace it would have served in hidden ways to give sufferers his strength and faith.

The lesson was clear – not to judge other people. It was a lesson I never mastered.

Some days later a mobile officers' shop made its appearance. I decided to buy a few things to alleviate the discomforts of the infernal desert. Resigned now to being a staff officer forever, I was subconsciously obeying an urge that always nudges me when depressed – to go out and buy something exciting, something on which to concentrate my being for a while instead of on my miseries. So I bought a camp-bed. Up to this I had always slept as my troops did, on the ground. But now I had no troops, so masochism was no longer necessary. I got a magnificent sleeping-bag, a pillow, and desert boots to replace my threadbare ones.

On the afternoon of 22 January 1943, the New Zealanders, supported by our tanks, began to move down from the hills towards Tripoli. I was sent with a message to Pete. As my jeep approached the battalion area I saw two officers standing on the road studying a map, one of them Henry, now commanding my troop. There was sporadic gunfire, no one taking much notice of it as the shells were passing over us towards some other target.

Suddenly I heard a different note, the metallic, deadly scream of an approaching shell. My driver and I flung ourselves onto the ground. Fragments of shell whirred close above our heads, so I knew it had landed on the road and not burrowed into the

soft verge. When we stood up there was little to be seen of
Henry and his companion. The shell had landed between them.

Next day, Tripoli was captured.

Troop Officer

I was ordered to rejoin the battalion and take over my troop
again. We were leaguered five miles from the city on a flat
grassy area which looked like reclaimed marshland. There
were several small dug-outs built by the Italians, some of
which we used as kitchens. Living quarters consisted of tents.

Returning from a visit to another regiment, I found myself
near Tripoli; though it was not yet in bounds for social visits, I
could not resist going in. It was disappointing, due in part to
the silence and emptiness, that temporary vacuum which
always followed the taking of towns. I bought eggs, cauliflow-
ers, carrots, onions and potatoes, consequently finding myself
extremely popular in the mess that evening. In Cairo I had
acquired some skill in haggling, but the Libyans were far harder to deal with. I had just enough Italian, Arabic, French and
English to be cheated in all four tongues.

A fortnight later Winston Churchill inspected a parade of
the Eighth Army in Tripoli. Like other formations we put out a
skeleton force, with one member appearing for each rank. I
was chosen to represent the subalterns. The parade was
impressive, lines and lines of troops standing smartly in front
of the white, sunlit buildings. Winston swept past in a staff car
returning our cheers and salutes in his usual vulgar manner.

Pete called us one day to an Orders Group. First, he summa-
rized the campaign so far and the lessons to be learnt from it
(Pete was naturally didactic), pointing out that, though the vice
was squeezing the enemy, there was still some hard fighting
ahead, particularly when we reached the hilly country and the
Mareth Line. Then, without apparent emotion, he surprised us
by expressing thanks for our loyalty and support – which he
would normally have taken for granted – and telling us that he
was leaving the battalion to take up a post in England. It meant
promotion to brigadier.

His successor was Lt Col I.F.M. Spence, a brilliant officer
with a warm personality. For my part, however, I was lost
without Pete. He gave me encouragement and confidence, both

of which I desperately needed, and despite his pomposity I felt he understood me. Believing I could succeed only under his patient and avuncular direction, I did not want to have to prove myself again and, as it happened, never had the same rapport with my subsequent CO.

A few weeks later, somewhat refreshed, we moved westwards for about a hundred miles, halting near Ben Gardane. We leaguered in a grove of trees, some in blossom, pink and white. There were olive trees too, lovely delicate things, all planted in rows with geometrical precision, so that whichever way you looked you saw an avenue. One night I decided to disdain my bivvy and my comfy camp-bed and sleep outside on the ground. When dawn came I watched an almond tree, in blossom, as the sun's rays struck its upper branches. It glowed, and in a few minutes the whole tree, like Moses's burning bush, seemed on fire. It thrilled me, the immediate beauty of it, but after a while I felt a great sense of loss, as though this tree represented all we were missing.

I was so tired of battle. My inner fear began to make me jumpy, the more so because it had to be hidden. Sudden noises made me duck. Sometimes, when shells were dropping nearby and splinters whistled past a few feet away, I felt in advance the jagged pain that would come with them into my torn flesh. At what point, I wondered, would the rejection take place, and in what form? My mind went back to Alamein, to Andy C., who had jumped out of his tank and run away. Now, I heard, he was a patient in the Psychiatric Unit. Strangely I always heard him spoken of with affection, never as a coward. Perhaps other people besides me could say in their hearts, 'There, but for the grace of God ... '

I had to do something to regain my poise. After all, apart from the shattering incident when I was wounded, I had been in battle very little compared to many others. I tried to learn to pray, regularly, not just in moments of fear, something I might never have done in milder circumstances. It was a curious experience. I never became very good at it, by which I mean I was never conscious of any reply. Two-way conversations with God seem to have come to an end with the prophets of the Old Testament. Of course there was Joan of Arc, but look what her voices led to. I accepted that my finite mind could not possibly understand the Infinite, yet I did on occasion have a sense of peace and comfort after trying to pray.

Some of my prayers were not very Christian, but they were fervent. Hate is a form of prayer. I hated the men who laid mines and booby-traps, who had killed several of my friends, because they killed coldly and deliberately, not in the heat of battle. Proximity in time and space often leads to twisted judgments. In retrospect I recognize that the aim in battle is to kill your enemy, and that ethically there is no difference between doing it with a mine and with a missile.

When we left Tripoli the new CO appointed me battalion navigator. This required considerable mathematical ability, which the Good Lord forgot to include when he dealt me his deck of talents. Converting grid and magnetic bearings, back bearings, checking mileages and so forth was most unconducive to my peace of mind. The responsibility was great, so I set to work familiarizing myself with the use of protractors, maps and God knows what, trying to remember what we'd been taught in the navigation course when we first arrived in Egypt. It seemed a very long time ago but the basics remained.

The most difficult times were after some of our 'Triumphal Entries' into towns along the route. The locals rushed up to our vehicles, cheering and clapping, offering us wines of various strengths and quality. When we'd gone through one biggish place – of which, perhaps understandably, I have forgotten the name – I felt that warfare in these conditions was more than tolerable. I noticed an indistinct haze which hadn't been there before. We emerged into tricky country and I began to experience moments of doubt and indecision. The CO kept coming up on the air with, 'Navigator, are you *sure* you know where we are?' And I would reply, 'Yes, yes, I'm quite happy about everything!' – which was true; I just hoped that his interpretation would be charitable. Luckily the enemy was miles away, and history records that we made our destination without error.

At this stage my troop was issued with armoured cars which had belonged to the South African Army in some bygone age. They were sleek and menacing in the way that a dead cobra is sleek and menacing. Grand old veterans of the Abyssinian campaign, they were totally unreliable. Apparently

our faithful dingoes had reached the end of their useful lives:
even so, they were aristocrats compared to their successors.

Laurel and Hardy

The battalion was being treated and refitted. The CO sent me
out early one morning to reconnoitre the area ahead, my chief
mission being to determine whether the texture of the sand, or
the 'going' as it was called, would be suitable for tanks.
Usually missions like this involved two cars but we had only
one, the others being too senile to operate.

We followed a wadi, dry and yellow-sided, for some miles,
a fairly deep one which hid us from detection. Finally we
emerged onto a great open plain and continued for another
mile. I halted to give my crew a rest. We made a brew of tea
and had some bully beef. It was very hot. A heat haze shim-
mering across the sand softened the glare to some extent.

The log was brought up to date and I was satisfied that
there was no more we could usefully do here. We were uncomfortably close to the enemy positions. I swept the area through
my binoculars once more and, seeing nothing but sand, gave
the order to mount and start up.

The car refused.

With the battery beginning its death throes I got on the air
and asked for help. We waited impatiently, hoping the enemy
would not spot us. The men began to get jumpy.

'Why the 'ell did they take away our dingoes and give us
these bloody contraptions?' my driver whined.

'Because', I started to reply patiently, when I realized he
wasn't listening. He was staring with idiotic disbelief at the
sand trail of a vehicle moving rapidly towards us. As it came
nearer, I saw it was a jeep, manned by a thin driver and a fat
passenger. They looked like Laurel and Hardy.

'Wot's the trouble, Sir?' demanded Hardy in an abrasive
tone, as though we were at fault in dragging him out to such
an unsavoury place. A fitter's place is properly in a workshop.

'Don't know. She won't start.'

'Huh.' They delved inside, muttering and cursing.

After I'd listened to them tinkering about for a while I called
out, 'Any idea what's wrong?'

'Electrical fault. System's wore out.'

At that moment a shell landed a few hundred yards due

west of us. Hardy peered startled out of the turret. Another shell landed a few hundred yards due east of us. Such a perfect bracket did not suggest random shelling.

'Cor! We're getting out of 'ere!' he yelled, raising his massive bulk.

'Oh no you're not,' I said, 'not till you've got this car going. You've got about a minute before we're hit, so you'd better work fast.'

He disappeared and worked fast. Surfacing a moment later he gasped, 'We've fixed it. Short circuit. You'll be OK now.'

He and his silent companion leapt into the jeep and drove wildly off. When they'd gone a short distance a shell landed behind them, like a farewell kick in the pants. Tears of laughter streamed down our faces.

'Never knew a jeep could move so fast!' my driver spluttered as we watched them, swerving from side to side, disappear behind their own trail of sand.

Hastily we mounted. 'Start up, driver,' I ordered with relief, 'turn her about and go like hell!'

Another shell landed, near enough for splinters to rattle on the sides of the car. Quickly he pressed the starter button.

The horn blew. We remained static. He pressed the starter again. Again the horn blew.

We clambered out as more shells exploded around us. It would be suicide to climb in now to radio for help, even if the set was working, which I doubted.

We began our sweaty march back. It was a long trek. We followed our wadi, becoming thirstier and thirstier, our water supply by now probably blown up in our crotchety car. The men spoke unkindly of the fitters.

Hours later we reached an area held by a very crack regiment. A smartly turned out sergeant escorted me to see the Second-in-Command, as I felt that being in such an advanced area he would appreciate my report. He was seated behind a desk in a square tent, the sort of unlikely structure one sees in pictures of medieval warfare. A few concubines lolling on silk cushions would not have been out of place. In fact there was one piece of furniture rarely seen in the desert, a long shelf supporting many bottles of alcoholic drinks. When I'd finished speaking, almost dead with exhaustion and thirst, my eyes were drawn towards these enticing containers. The Major caught my glance, looked at his watch, and said, 'Bit early for a dwink, what?'

It was ten minutes to six.

Impressed by his reverence for the legal opening time I saluted and withdrew. Outside, the sergeant, whose hearing must have been very acute, whispered, 'Come with me, Sir. We'll 'ave a drink in the sergeants' mess.'

'Sergeant,' I said gratefully, 'just now there's nothing I'd like more than a dwink – er – drink.'

El Hamma

A few days later the Eighth Army launched its famous attack on the Mareth Line. Monty's plan was a frontal assault while the New Zealanders, heavily reinforced, swept south and west on a 150-mile left hook to trap the enemy behind the Line. We were part of the heavy reinforcements.

Our tanks were loaded onto transporters. It was a dusty march, carried out mainly by night. No lights were allowed, and there was wireless silence. I began now to think benevolently of our tyrannous English master at Repton, who made us learn by heart most of Shakespeare's *Julius Caesar* and Milton's *Comus*. Calpurnia's words to Caesar when she tried to persuade him not to go to the Capitol were particularly apt:

> Fierce fiery warriors fought upon the clouds,
> In ranks and squadrons and right form of war,
> Which drizzled blood upon the Capitol;
> The noise of battle hurtled in the air,
> Horses did neigh, and dying men did groan ...

Repeating such marvellous lines to myself was an excellent substitute for reading and I found that the constant repetition suggested meanings I'd never perceived before. This alleviated the tedium of trundling through the darkness, and the effort required kept me awake, something my squadron leader naturally expected.

We rounded the Matmata massif, twenty-two miles inland, to which the Mareth Line extended, and headed for the narrow gap between the Jebels Melab and Tebaga, leading to El Hamma. The letters RR printed on our maps at the low slopes at each end of the opening stood for Roman Ruins, and between them, extending from one to the other, was shown a Roman wall.

Tactically, then, nothing had changed since the days when the Romans protected their African territory against raiders from the south. These little forts were in visual contact and passage through the gap was impeded by the wall and the soldiers manning it, as well as by the missiles hurled from the over-looking forts. Now, in 1943, the Germans were using the same tactic of guarding the gap, but with distant, long-range artillery, the modern equivalent of Roman spears, arrows and catapults.

On 25 March we approached the gap and occupied some high ground on the right. About a quarter of a mile ahead of our leaguer was a conical hill, 200 feet high, which I was now sent to investigate. The South African cars were now proved useless, and I was given a jeep instead. In this tenacious little car we were able to drive almost to the summit. The first thing we saw was a rough cable made of many strands of flex leading to a well-concealed, man-made hollow. There was no doubt what this was: a forward observation post, with a clear view of the plain we had crossed, and from which the enemy artillery, positioned miles away behind the hills, could be directed.

The prospect of exploring this dug-out was not attractive – even if deserted it was probably booby-trapped – but in the circumstances we had no choice. If this post was still operative it would not be long before shells began raining down on the battalion area. I edged in, followed by my driver, Trooper Brown, with the Bren. The air was stale and smelled earthy. There was a solid and permanent quality to this dug-out which suggested that it was unlikely to be abandoned without very good cause. Down we went, stopping every step to listen, expecting all the time to be torn apart by a hidden explosive. Half-way in Brown nudged me: the wires, which led loosely from the opening, were cut at this point. Almost certain now that the post was deserted I saw no good in proceeding and getting uselessly shot by waiting men if my surmises were not correct. What light there was would be behind, outlining us as perfect targets.

The danger seemed no longer from men but from booby-traps. Taking half-steps, examining the floor and walls for any suspicious items, we withdrew gingerly back up the stairs. At the top I looked carefully out and immediately froze. Two figures in Italian uniforms were creeping on hands and knees towards us. They hadn't seen me, but in a few seconds they were going to. Making a silent signal to Brown to follow me, I rushed out across the ten yards or so that separated us. Taken by surprise they threw their hands up, and Brown disarmed them. They were big men, their uniforms scruffy and too heavy for the desert, and both wore large untidy beards.

We made them kneel. I took the Bren while Brown searched them. As I watched him my fingers fondled the gun, familiar-iz-ing themselves with its touch and balance. Suddenly it came apart. Surprised, but unworried, I ignored this small event as I watched, spellbound, one of the most comic histrionic acts it has ever been my privilege to see. There they knelt, these two gigantic men, their hands aloft, while tears cascaded down their cheeks, converged at the lowest points of their beards, and dripped heavily onto the sand.

'Mamma mia! Mamma mia!' they wailed, adding further invocations to the celestial hierarchy. The effect, which was intended to be pathetic, and would have been in the case of a pair of infants recently orphaned, was extremely entertaining. Consequently my would-be secret attempts to fit the two parts of the Bren together again lacked the necessary concentration, and to my embarrassment I dropped part of the little gun. One of the prisoners, in mid Mamma-mia, made a dive for it, but got such a kick in the rump from Brown that he stopped with a yelp. I took over guard duty while Brown reassembled the gun, and sensed his humorous contempt for someone who couldn't handle a simple sub-machine-gun. When he'd fin-ished he smirked and said with tolerant authority, 'Never trust a Wop, Sir!'

That night was noisy as an endless armada of bombers roared overhead and the reverberation of their bombs in the narrow valley returned to assault our ears. How could human beings endure, even survive, such thunderbolts? Surely our attack next day would be a bloodless formality.

Throughout the next morning the bombing continued. Under cover of a sandstorm we moved into our position. Linking once more with the distant past the tanks of all three brigade regiments lined up on the remains of the Roman wall, now no more than a bank a foot high. It was a rare and astonishing sight. Between the hills, stretching right across the gap, stood seventy tanks, their engines growling, fifty yards apart. Behind them another seventy, and behind them infantry on foot and in carriers. On the back of each tank crouched two or three New Zealand infantry.

We were to advance in line abreast; there would be no stopping, whatever the opposition. An hour before we started, the artillery put down another crunching barrage.

At 4 p.m. the order was given to advance. Slowly, inexorably, the first wave moved forward, the roar of engines mingling with the sound of guns and bombs. The storm had abated, but the tracks churned up the layers of dust. Not being a member of a tank crew I remained behind in my jeep, ready for any assignment the CO might have for me. The sight of the great grey machines lumbering through the semi-darkness was terrifying. Its effect on the enemy became clear an hour later when rows of Italian soldiers scrambled out from a network of trenches, their hands up, to surrender. As they came towards us we saw that the German troops behind them, not approving of their allies' lack of fibre, were firing at their backs. We had no objection to such a curious form of civil war.

This battle, one of the greatest set-piece battles in the history of warfare, went exactly according to plan. The Germans, stunned but determined, gave rugged resistance. At one point we were ordered to halt. Although casualties had been severe we not only achieved our objective but penetrated beyond it. The enemy had good reason to suspect that a lull must follow now. But suddenly through the gloom appeared the van of another huge tank force, the 1st Armoured Division. They drove through our now static lines, and continued to the northern end of the valley, a distance of about 6000 yards, where they had to halt as darkness fell. When the moon rose they advanced again, cleaving through the enemy formations, which included the formidable 21st Panzer Division.

I was now sent to add my iota to the mopping up after this mighty conflict, which had taken place in so narrow a defile. The moon shed a macabre brightness, accentuating some features, distorting others. Standing on a brilliantly lit surface, I became conscious of the obvious target I presented, flopped onto my hands and knees and stared into the black depth of an open trench. I could hear no movement. Leaving my driver to guard the jeep I clambered down. A cold air struck my skin. Like the First World War trenches this one was built in a zig-zag. Cautiously I crept along, keeping close to the side, making as little noise as possible. Rounding a corner I recoiled in horror, stepping on a board as I did so. The cracking seemed to fill the universe. I was face to face with a German in the classic kneeling position, his rifle aimed straight at my chest. I took another step back, pointing my revolver at the spot where he would appear, my body tense, trying to silence my breathing. I envisaged the man, the highly trained soldier, caressing the trigger, smiling perhaps, his face drawn as I had seen it, thin-lipped, pale in the shadows. Fear paralysed my will. If I didn't act soon he would attack me, and I would be helpless. There was no question of running away. The moment he heard me move he would step out and shoot me in the back. Or he would follow me until I tried to climb out of the trench, killing me with cold efficiency. In either case my death would not merit any medals.

Terror can beget courage. Levelling my revolver I stepped around the corner and shouted '*Hände hoch!*' He didn't move. His rifle was now pointing above my left shoulder, but that could be a ruse. I watched him carefully. Again I ordered him to put his hands up, and again there was no response. He was very dead.

I removed his rifle and searched his pockets. There was no sign of a wound; he must have been killed by the blast of a bomb or an exploding shell. He was dead for only a few hours, but already the sweet, nauseating smell infected the air.

The final chapter of the North African campaign was now beginning. The immediate aim was to capture the ports of Sfax and Sousse, so that the Eighth Army could land the supplies it needed for the advance to Tunis.

Our next engagement was at the Wadi Akarit, a battle of which I retain only the vaguest memory, except that we suffered heavy casualties. At nightfall we withdrew into leaguer on a forward slope, a quarter of a mile behind the Gabe's-Gafsa road. Mac was recruiting help from able-bodied men to deal with the wounded. As the night progressed more tanks came in, off-loading battered men, some savagely torn, some so badly hurt that all he could do was give them morphia to help them die as painlessly as possible.

I was applying bandages to a wounded corporal when I was summoned to RHQ. I was to be the leading officer in a Dramatic Event. An American unit from the First Army was approaching along the road from the west. The first contact in actual battle between the two armies, and indeed between the Allies, would take place in our sector. I was to drive out to meet them. As I left, the CO said drily, 'Try not to get shot up!'

We drove in low gear down the hill, skirting as best we could in the dark the hollows and outcrops. To get onto the road itself we had to negotiate a ditch which ran alongside it. As we motored slowly westward I began to realize the import of the CO's parting admonition. How exactly does one make contact with an ally on a lonely road in the middle of the night? Stride forward, left hand on gat, right hand extended for the historic handshake, friendly grin on face, and exclaim, 'Uncle Sam, I presume'? There should be a team of cameramen ready to record the great moment. I wondered if the Americans had been told to expect nothing more than a lone captain in a jeep. I asked Brown how he thought we should set about our task. His answer was not reassuring.

'From wot I've 'eard, Sir, the Yanks is a bit trigger-'appy after the bashing they got at Kasserine. Nah it's shoot first and ask questions after.'

Just then a red glow appeared ahead. I told Brown to pull off onto what looked like flat ground on the right and we proceeded slowly, keeping twenty yards from the verge, hoping the enemy had sown no mines here. The glow was now transformed into jagged flames writhing up into the sky, deep red roaring flames. A row of bushes and small trees, vivid in the flickering light, forced us away from the edge. We inched towards the inferno, which was coming from two Bren carriers parked side by side in the middle of the narrow road, rendering it impassable. But who had set them on fire, friend or foe? And why?

Before I could think further a voice from the ditch on our left bellowed, 'Halt! Who goes there?' The crackling of the flames made it difficult to know just where the voice was coming from.

'Friend!' I shouted, dismounting hastily.

'Advance, friend, and be recognized!'

'How the hell can I advance when I don't know where you are!'

'Just put your bloody hands up and keep walking.'

I took a few paces forward and peered into the ditch. It was deep.

'We've got you covered – keep moving!'

'OK. But when I jump don't think I'm trying to rush you.'

'Wouldn't do you much good, mate.'

I couldn't see how wide or how deep the ditch was.

Sick with terror I took a flying leap into the darkness. As I landed and scrambled to my feet a rifle was pushed into my stomach.

'Who are you?'

I gave my name and rank, hoping this wasn't a section of English-speaking Germans, and was at once surrounded by a group of men, whose blackened faces, grotesque in the light of the flames, I recognized as being from the infantry under our command.

'It's all right, men,' came a voice from the shadows, 'I know this officer.' A tall figure came forward, an amused grin splitting his face. He laughed throughout our conversation, evidently finding the situation in general, and me in particular, a huge joke.

'You're a lucky so-and-so. We had one Bren and five rifles trained on you and your driver, ho, ho! We've knocked out three vehicles already, and killed their crews, ho, ho, ho!'

'What saved me, then?'

'We thought we'd like a change and take the next lot prisoner instead of shooting them, ho, ho! And you behaved differently, so we thought you might not be enemy. You didn't switch on your lights or try to get past the road-block. Three Huns tried to. You can see their cars and their bodies over there, ho, ho!'

'Thanks.' I preferred not to look.

A nauseating bile rose in my throat. I wasn't to know the criteria by which these men had chosen to decide who should live and who should die. It was by sheer luck that we were still alive.

'Thanks, Hugh,' I said again. 'I'd better get back and tell the CO you're here and what you're doing.'

'No need. We're acting under his orders. Would you take this Hun back – our only survivor, ho, ho! – and ask Mac to look after him?'

A German officer was led towards me, his left eye dangling half-way down his cheek. Clenching my teeth to avoid puking I put him aboard the jeep.

'Follow that star,' said Hugh, 'it'll take you straight back to battalion. No mines.'

Brown supported the German as I drove. He was very weak. After a bumpy ride we reached the leaguer and went directly to Mac's vehicle.

'I've got a badly wounded German officer here, Mac.'

'He'll fucking well have to die,' he answered sharply. 'I've too many of our own chaps to deal with.'

Mac was exhausted. He had worked for hours, and went on working all that night. Next morning I watched a small convoy of prisoners being driven away, among them our one-eyed friend, his head neatly bandaged. Mac was the gruffest Christian I'd ever met.

The Prisoner

We advanced steadily northwards. The enemy, retreating towards the hills, sandwiched between us and the First Army, was constantly probing our positions and, whenever he could, offering fierce opposition.

One evening, about 4 p.m., the battalion began to occupy the area in which we were to leaguer that night. In front of us was a gentle rise sweeping in a wide arc, its arms curving away from us to the north. One squadron was detailed to set up on the crest, hull down, and I was to go with them. All was quiet, no movement, no planes, no sign of the enemy in any form. Below us lay the valley and beyond that, a mile away, a series of graded hills. The air was still. Relaxed, we smoked and chatted and enjoyed the deep green and purple colours of the vegetation, so pleasant after the hundreds of miles of hot-smelling sand.

Suddenly a movement was seen. All binoculars focused on the spot, some distance away among the foothills. At first it was impossible to see what was moving, but a picture emerged as tank commanders came up on the air with new information.

'It's a vehicle – can't make out what sort – it seems to be swanning around – '

'It's heading towards us now. Looks like an armoured car.'

'Seems to be on its own. Can't see any support.'

We watched intently as it veered out onto the level ground and nosed slowly in our direction, halting every now and again while its commander searched the area through his binoculars.

'It's German all right. Something new – never seen one like it before. Shall I shoot it up?'

'No,' came the Squadron Leader's voice, 'let him come on. We'll shoot him when he gets closer, when I say so.'

On he came, oblivious of the fact that at least ten armour-piercing guns were trained on him. At 200 yards he stopped. He must have seen or sensed us there, because the car started to reverse.

'Fire one!' ordered the Squadron Leader.

There was the report of a single round. The commander slewed sideways in the turret, raised himself with difficulty and put up his arms in surrender. The car appeared not to be hit.

It was my job, followed by a detachment of infantry in a Bren carrier, to take him prisoner. He was very young, fair-haired, wearing the black cap with flat top rising high above the peak which was standard wear for German officers in Europe. The fact that he was wearing it now suggested that he was newly arrived in the Afrika Corps and not yet fitted out with desert kit. He was very pale.

He stood blinking at me in the glare of sunlight. His left hand gripped the rim of the turret, his right remained inside it. Thinking he might be holding a weapon I waited till the infantry arrived and then told him to dismount. There was a moment of tension as he used his left hand to raise the right, an expression of controlled agony on his face. There was no right hand. It had been shot off at the wrist; blood was still spurting from the stump.

We got him out of the car and Brown applied a bandage while I searched his pockets. Apart from routine documents

there were two items which riveted my attention. One was a
photograph of a village street in Russia, very wide, like those
in Ireland. In the middle was a gibbet, a peasant hanging from
it by the neck. Round this pathetic corpse stood a group of
grinning German officers. A small inked asterisk indicated our
prisoner. On the back was another asterisk, and in German the
words 'This is me!'

The other item was a little black notebook, containing verses
pencilled in our friend's handwriting.

> Early in the morning, before sunrise,
> The patrol has long since awakened,
> And goes against the enemy.
> Proudly their cars drive in the morning breeze.
> No bird sings its song.
> No – everything is bleak and desolate.
> Heavily the car finds its way through the sand
> And disappears behind a hill
> To take cover.

Those lines, which no doubt sound better in their original
German, ring true to anyone in an armoured unit who has
taken part in an early morning action.

Next there was something more personal, a little pathetic:

> A mother, full of grief and sorrow,
> Fears for her only son.
> Her son, far away from his country,
> Fighting for his Fatherland.

Finally, a few unfinished lines expressing the hopelessness
of the Germans as defeat became inevitable:

> From early morning until late at night
> The thunder of the guns.
> Against an overwhelming force ...

It has been said that in every German there is a dreamer and
a brute.

Enfidaville

There was a fierce battle for the Enfidaville position. The New
Zealanders attacked at night, storming the high ground. The
tanks were to follow up next morning.

We bedded down early in the open. I was persecuted by
squadrons of mosquitoes, coming down like miniature dive-

bombers, piercing the skin sharply and painfully. I put my head deeper in my sleeping-bag, applied as much anti-mozzie ointment as I could, and hopefully emerged. In a way the result was worse than being stung, because I could hear them zooming down and hovering when they got the smell of the ointment. There was an age of suspense as one waited for attack or withdrawal.

The noise of battle echoed in the hills. Unable to sleep I became more and more tense. Writhing about, trying to ignore the mozzies, and living again the engagements of the past weeks, a mood of hopelessness enveloped me. Always before a battle the thought exists that one may be killed, yet a paradoxical and illogical conviction of one's immortality overlays it. On this occasion the thought became a certainty. Having accepted what I believed to be a presentiment, I felt a deep calm pervading me, as though of welcome. I hoped it would be a brief and painless end. I hoped the news would not be too devastating for those I loved at home. And yet, and yet, as I dramatized, did I also hope, deep down, that I must if possible spare them this sorrow?

At dawn we lined up in a steep-sided wadi for our advance into the hills. Heavy gunfire was coming from the direction of Takrouna. Seeing Mac's vehicle nearby I walked over to him, wanting to tell him about my presentiment.

'Just a death-wish,' he said flatly, raising his cup of tea to his mouth, draining it, and then pressing his lips together into a straight dismissive line.

'What are you talking about, Mac? I don't want to die!'

'It just means you're in a funk, looking for a way of escape. Happens to lots of chaps.' He handed his mug to an orderly and boarded his car.

Thoughtfully I returned to my jeep. He could be right. In a strange way his bluntness helped. I didn't like to think I was more frightened than anyone else.

A sudden stonk of 88-millimetre shells prevented further introspection. We began to move in line ahead, snaking slowly uphill. The wadi was steep and narrow, and at one point there was a delay as a tank with a damaged track was shifted to the side. A figure in a greatcoat lay on the platform behind the turret.

'Someone overslept?' I called out facetiously.

'No, Sir. It's the Sergeant-Major. He's dead.'

It was becoming lighter when we emerged onto a plateau, green and brown, edged with outcrops of white rock and circled by low hills. The tanks took up positions facing north, where a low gap gave a vista of hills and valleys stretching into the distance. The infantry of the 6th New Zealand Brigade, under whose command we now operated, were hidden from us on both sides. The hills shone vivid in the sharp early morning sunlight, an ironic scene of peacefulness.

I was now attached to RHQ. There was nothing for me to do but enjoy the view, as I was doing when told to go to the NZ HQ on our right, ascertain their immediate intentions both for us and for themselves, and arrange recognition signals. Leaving the plateau I descended eastwards over fields crisscrossed by rough walls which reminded me of the West of Ireland, although these were whiter, being built of the local quartz. As we eased down the slope these walls became so frequent that I sent the jeep back to battalion and continued alone on foot.

There was no difficulty in finding the NZ HQ. The Major in charge was marking my map when a shell landed nearby. I flung myself to the ground. When I looked up I saw that all the New Zealand officers were standing. What is more, they were laughing. The OC said with a chuckle, 'Looks like someone's a bit windy!'

Humiliated, I started the short return journey up the hill, scrambling over the walls, pondering Mac's remarks about my being bomb-happy. The way I had just reacted bore out his diagnosis. On the other hand, despite my premonition, this was too lovely a day on which to die. The clear mountain air smelling of grass, scented slightly by the tang of the sea and of hot earth, was something to relish, something to banish fear and morbidity. The struggle of life versus death was swinging strongly in favour of life.

My mood having undergone this transition, I was singing happily as I stepped over the last outcrop of rock onto the plateau. The sun was brilliant, a flash reflecting off the talc covering my map. The tanks were static, the whole scene like a painting in its stillness and serenity.

Maybe the enemy spotted the flash of light and deduced that there were troops on the hidden plateau, for an airburst immediately above us was followed by an explosion in our midst. I flung myself to the ground for the second time that day. But this was no stray shell: it was a battery shot of extreme accuracy. I wriggled towards a Sherman tank, trying to find shelter behind it. As I moved two things happened. First I felt a thump on my right calf, then the tank started to reverse. Rolling out of its way, I screamed for the commander, who couldn't see me, and again when he turned, the tracks grinding up the earth as he reversed once more in my direction. I kept on screaming even though nothing could be heard above the din of stick after stick of shells. All the time I was futilely trying to protect my head, my stomach, my genitals, the most sensitive and vulnerable parts of the body, by covering them with my arms and curling myself up into a foetal position.

I alternated between trying desperately to escape from the tracks of the tank, and scrabbling for refuge in the too solid earth with my fingernails. Had people not more pressing matters to keep their eyes on, they would have been transported by this sorry, comical performance. At last the tank stopped manoeuvring. An ache in my leg made me look down. The whole of the right trouser-leg was soaked in blood. Another stonk shattered the air, fragments of metal spraying out, menacing the flesh. But this time I didn't seem to care. The pain wasn't too bad as drowsiness began to bring me peace.

A distant voice called. It belonged to a trooper in my squadron; his face was familiar but I couldn't remember his name. It worried me that I was meeting him off duty and couldn't address him by name. He was kneeling beside a jeep. Curious kind of behaviour. I hadn't seen him salute.

'Come on, Sir, quick as you can!'

Another loud crash nearby. He was giving me some sort of order, which wasn't right: it's the officer who gives the orders.

'All right, leave it to me.' He lifted me up and put me in his jeep.

The noise continued loudly, then grew less as we dipped over the hill. I was coming to when we reached the armoured medical vehicle. Mac, his lips pursed in that manner which always made me feel I'd said or done something stupid, disappeared into his car, emerging a moment later with an enormous pair of scissors.

'What's that for, Mac?'

'Cut off your leg, you bloody fool.' Resigned, I closed my eyes. 'Hm. Nice Blighty one,' he added.

I looked down. He had cut off the trouser-leg from the thigh, washed the wound and was bandaging it.

'What do you mean?'

'I mean you've got a flesh wound that'll keep you out of battle for a while. Can't tell how much damage there is. You got what you wanted, didn't you?'

'Well ... er ... thanks, Mac!'

'Oh shut up!' I was bundled into an ambulance as he turned to deal with another casualty.

Some months later I learnt that my rescuer had been awarded the Military Medal.

SIX

Casualty Clearing Station

Pleasantly drugged by the shot Mac had given me, I surrendered entirely to the sense of relief, of safety, and, above all, of comfort.

I was dozing off when the engine started. There were no bunks in this ambulance, and I lay on a stretcher. The orderly sat in front with the driver; this didn't worry me, I was so sleepy. An explosion outside reminded me that we were still in the battle zone. It also reminded the driver, who put his foot down so hard that the vehicle shot forward like a stone from a catapult. Another burst of gunfire, another burst of speed. There was no road here, and I deduced that we were taking the shortest route to get out of range. My deduction proved correct when we hit a bump and I was thrown into the air, landing painfully on the floor. I tried to roll back onto the stretcher but another bump lofted me again towards the ceiling. I yelled to the driver but he didn't hear me, or preferred not to. My leg was bleeding again, my body sore all over with the force of impact as I hit the floor. Realizing there was no hope of attracting attention, a terrible helplessness came over me. What a way to die, buffeted to death in an ambulance, alone, at the will of a cowardly driver and an orderly who was too frightened to perform his duty to the patient. I was reaching the point of despair when there was a change of sound from the wheels and we began to run smoothly. The road led to a casualty clearing station, run by New Zealanders.

They put my stretcher down in a corner of the tent. An orderly gave me a packet of cigarettes and a bar of chocolate.

'Now, Sir, if you don't mind, a few questions. Name? Number? Rank? Nature of wound – let's see – gunshot, right leg. OK, Sir? Quite comfortable? I'll get you some tea.'

I lit one of the Red Cross cigarettes and looked round the
tent. It was rectangular, big enough to hold twenty casualties.
The air smelled of hot canvas, disinfectants, anaesthetic and
sweaty bodies. Most of the wounded were New Zealanders,
tanned and cheerful. They were laughing at a story being told
by a fair-haired officer in the corner:

'... near Sousse. Bags of wine. Div. HQ was just off the road,
there was hundreds of civvies, Wogs an' Frogs, all crowdin'
round the General.'

General Sir Bernard Freyberg vc, popularly known as 'Tiny'
in ironical reference to his great stature, commanded all New
Zealand troops in the Middle East.

'Tiny was tellin' 'em – '

Here a new stretcher-case was brought in and I lost part of
the story.

' ... suddenly there's a noise at the back of the crowd, an' a
Bren carrier comes through, with a couple of privates in it. The
one standin' up was swayin' about and yellin', "Anyone know
where we are? Where the muckin' hell are we?" Suddenly his
eye lights on the General. He leaps out and staggers up to Tiny,
who doesn't see him comin', slaps him on the back an' says,
"Ho, General! Can you tell us where we are? Bet you muckin'
can't!" Tiny turns round, an' the crowd is very quiet. At first he
looks very stern, but all he says is, "I think someone's had too
much liquor!" and smiles. So they hustles the fella away quickly, an' Tiny goes on addressin' the crowd as if nothing had
happened.'

It was refreshing to be among these Kiwis, with their
clipped speech, their informality and spontaneous sense of fun,
their courage and loyalty to the great General Freyberg. A New
Zealand sergeant told me that after the attack on El Hamma
Tiny paraded some fifty Italian officers, prisoners of war, and
berated them soundly for laying down their arms. Officers, he
said, should remember their responsibilities to their men. They
were leaders, they must always bear in mind the professional
prestige of the officer and fight to the end, whatever their feeling for their cause, or however hopeless their position might
seem.

'Course,' the Sergeant added without a flicker, 'course, Tiny
gets real wild if he don't get a fight!'

After that battle some of us were introduced to Tiny. He towered above everyone, not only physically but in that vast personality. It took two days to recover from his bone-crushing handshake.

The orderly came back with a mug of tea. I tried to sit up to drink but found it difficult. My leg was aching. The officer on the stretcher next to mine held the mug while I manoeuvred myself onto my side.

'Where'd you get it, Pommie?'

'In the right calf, Kiwi.'

'OK now?'

'OK.'

'Were ya in that tank that brewed up in the wadi?'

'No. I was on my way back from your lot with a message. It was HE. What happened to you?'

'Bullet in the leg.'

'Where? Takrouna?'

'In the hills to the east. The Ities were holding a pass with machine-guns. They killed my sergeant and three men, and wounded me and several others. When we got near they got windy and put their hands up. We went in and finished the job off with grenades.'

'No prisoners?'

'Not bloody likely! They kill you from a safe position and when it gets too hot they give themselves up. Too bloody easy.'

'Who was it took two machine-gun nests single-handed?' boomed a serious voice from the other side.

'Me!' said the fair-haired officer.

'With a walkin'-stick!' added my friend.

Another stretcher was brought in and carried to a space at the far end. Every head followed it, trying to recognize the occupant.

'Hullo, Bill! What got you?'

No answer.

'He's out, Sir. Head wound.'

'I see.'

There was a silence. I found myself dozing off.

It was pleasant here after the stress of battle, pleasant to lie back and allow others to make decisions, to take a rest. The

ache in my leg was increasing despite the shot the doctor had
given me. The wound didn't look much, but I'd lost a lot of
blood. I wondered how many others in the battalion had been
clanged too: things seemed to be getting pretty sticky when I
was hit.

My thoughts switched to home. I must try to let them know
I'm all right before the official telegram arrives, that bleak
statement: 'The Army Council regrets to inform you that
Captain ... ' The sort of communication you start to read, then
catch your breath to gather strength for the last part.

God, it's hot in here. This morning, early, before the sun was
up, the Sergeant-Major was killed. We passed his tank in the
wadi and, thinking he was asleep on the back of it, I called out
to him. But he was dead. The eyes of his crew were scared. So
was I. Did I show it? God, how lucky I'd been – or was there a
design in these things? There can't be. It's chaos, death scat-
tered like rice at a wedding. And pain, pain in the body and
the mind. And there are those at home one loves. What are
they doing now? They don't know about me, don't know I'm
safe for a bit. Listening to the news, dreading the postman's
knock and the telephone's ring, they are suffering now, and
will suffer after me, until that telegram arrives. Be with them,
dear God. Be with all wounded men. Be with the friends and
relatives of the dead. There is no comfort for them ... no comfort ... no ...

Someone was groaning. A mist of unconsciousness came
down, cleared for a time, and came down again. Fitfully I
swam into forgetfulness, but forgot no more than my immediate surroundings, my whole being throbbing to the beat of battle. I could not rest.

Next day they took me into the operating theatre, which was
a tent. On another table lay an officer with a gaping hole in his
throat, rimmed by some silver-coloured stuff that looked like
mercury. A group of surgeons leant over him, one of them
prodding at the wound. I closed my eyes in horror. Some kind
person took advantage of my temporary blindness, and I felt a
jab in my arm.

When I woke up I was back in the ward. My leg was in plaster from the knee down to my toes, which peeped out like
white mice. An orderly gave me the piece of shrapnel they'd

extracted. Jagged, about the size of a large marble, it had steered a lucky course, missing all the important nerves, muscles, bones and blood vessels, just failing to emerge on the other side. The surgeon completed its journey to exit.

Despite the sedatives, and the care and concern of the New Zealand medical staff, sleep was impossible because of the groaning and tormented cries of men at night, as well as the turmoil in my mind.

My relief was great when I was put on a small plane to be flown to hospital in Tripoli. I was the only passenger, and lay snugly comfortable on a stretcher. It was good to see my kit being put on board. I began to doze off. Was I dreaming, or were they removing my kit? Fully awake I asked what the hell they were doing.

'Orders, Sir. Senior officer coming aboard. Only room for one kit, so it has to be his.'

Knowing the risks of being separated from one's kit in a battle zone I cursed loudly. In a moment a senior officer bounded aboard. He wore a purple band on his cap, which meant that he was a very senior padre. He ignored me.

We took off, flying over orchards and vineyards at tree-top height to avoid enemy fighters. The drone of the engine made me drowsy; at last, after all those sleepless days and nights I gave in to delicious oblivion.

A voice sounded above me, which I tried not to hear. Then a hand was shaking my shoulder. It was the Padre. With a professional grin he asked me how I felt. In language unbecoming an officer and a gentleman I told him to bugger off. He looked hurt, but left me in peace. I am sure he meant well.

I was glad of that sleep because for the whole of the first night in hospital I was kept awake by the screams of the officer in the next bed. It was a hideous noise, alternately rousing exasperation and compassion. At last someone gave him a sedative.

Next morning he apologized. 'Did I keep you awake?'

'Well, yes. What was the matter?'

'Could you bear it if ... '

'Go on.'

Hesitantly, in broken phrases, his voice sometimes sinking to inaudibility, sometimes rising stridently, he told me what had happened. He was in a Gurkha Regiment, second-in-command of a company. They put in a dawn attack at Akarit. The enemy were entrenched behind their defences, but the Gurkhas managed to scramble over and attack them hand to hand. Some Italians put up their hands in surrender. 'Their hands', he went on, 'were – they didn't look right, their fists were clenched. As we got near they opened them and threw some bombs – little ones, plastic. They killed several of my Gurkhas and wounded others. This made the men mad ... have you ever seen Gurkhas in a rage? They drew their kukris and charged, slashing off hands and arms and ... and heads. Suddenly, when I realized what the Ities had done I saw red too ...' He repeated in a whimper, 'I saw red too ... I seized a kukri off one of the dead men and waded in. Can't remember much, except that I ... decapitated ... at least one man. When it was all over the awful truth of what I'd done struck me and, I don't know, I just couldn't take it. I was wounded, but not badly. Now – I can't get it out of my mind – all that blood and the heads rolling about in the dust – Christ! – and I'd cut one of them off ... '

His face was twisted. He covered his head in his hands and started weeping. At last he fell asleep.

Egypt Again

Sitting in a dentist's chair happens comparatively seldom in an average lifetime, which is fortunate. Yet the anticipations and fears are so intense that it feels as though the period between visits had never been, and this visit were simply a continuation of the previous one.

As I lay in the hospital ward in Cairo I had a similar feeling of *déjà vu*. The events between now and my last spell in hospital seemed no more than a dream. Here was the cheerful efficiency of the nursing sisters, and the apparent callousness of senior officers.

On arrival we were put into a large, dark ward, and inspected by the senior medical officer, a colonel. When he came to me he tore off the label the New Zealand surgeon had attached to my plaster, which gave details of my wound and operation, and threw it away without reading it. Then viciously he tweaked one of my toes.

'Ow!' I yelled.

'Good! That means your leg's all right!'

When he'd finished his round he said to the Ward Sister, 'No interesting cases in this lot.'

The man who has been in battle and survived is intensely alive, intensely egotistical. His senses are taut. The shattering tumult of battle, the fears, the death of comrades, the agony of wounds, are fresh in his mind. To himself he is the most interesting being in the world. To the doctor he is just another case, and only the very worst cases are now of medical interest. Such professional detachment is desolation to the wounded.

When I'd been in hospital for five weeks the plaster was removed from my leg and I was sent to the same convalescent depot as before. The army is just to those who suffer in its causes and looks after them well, but it never lets them forget that they are drawing the sovereign's pay. So it followed that as I became more mobile I was given light duties, such as inspecting the guard, censoring the letters, and, later, those of orderly officer. For some reason my leg was healing very slowly, which was frustrating. My fellow convalescents, though fun, were from other units, so our relationship was bound to be temporary, never developing beyond the stage of *bonhomie*.

I was glad, therefore, to learn that Andy C. was in a psychiatric hospital nearby. I longed to see him again but there were problems, not the least being that of transport. I explained the problem to the Adjutant, who laid on a truck, with driver, for a whole day.

My feelings were confused as I waited in an ante-room. What was I going to find? A vegetable? A man so crippled with shame that he wouldn't want to meet an old friend? Would he, in fact, be recognizable as the Andy I had known?

At length I was summoned by a member of the staff, a major, who told me that, while Andy's lively character was a help, recovery was bound to be slow. On the surface he was as normal as anyone but the wound to his mind was deep. His self-esteem had suffered, and he acted wildly at times to reassert it. Periods of depression alternated with others of excessive elation. The real healer was time, helped initially by drugs.

'Of course you may take him out,' he said, 'but avoid any

excitements, such as cabarets. Don't let him out of your sight.
Above all, no alcohol – the reaction with the drugs would be
incalculable. If you've any difficulties ring me at once. And have
him back by six o'clock.'

During the drive to Port Said Andy chatted happily. He
wanted news of everyone in the battalion. Never once did he
refer to his own situation.

We found a pleasant restaurant and settled down to coffee.
Andy looked much the same, a little thinner, his eyes paler
than I remembered them. At first he was reserved, looking
round as though quietly relishing his freedom. Gradually he
became more vivacious, more like the merry companion I'd
known before.

Stories, often against himself, came bubbling out.

'You know I'm an agnostic. Hadn't been in church for years
when I joined up. Forgotten all the rules, like taking your hat
off, and so on. So my first Church Parade was quite an event.
An ignorant sergeant told us to get fell in, C of E to the right,
RCs to the left, Other Denominations to the rear – you know
the drill – and we were marched off to our respective churches.
I had a seat by the aisle. Before the service the Sergeant strutted
up and down as though he were on the parade-ground. Suddenly he stopped and stared at me. I knew there was something wrong with my dress but couldn't make out what. He
swelled up like a bullfrog and bellowed, "Don't you know better than to wear your bloody 'at in the 'Ouse of God?"'

Andy chuckled. 'The Sarge must have been deeply religious!' he said.

The laughter faded from his eyes. Their blueness became
opaque as he stared across the tables.

'Andy,' I said. Silence. 'Andy!' Again silence.

Then he shook his head and stood up. 'I must have a pee.'

He strode across the floor, leaving me reflecting on this dramatic change of mood. Time passed. I became worried. Then I
remembered the Major's instructions, 'Don't let him out of
your sight.' Oh my God! I rushed over to the Gents, but he
wasn't there. I paid the bill and hurried out onto the pavement.

The heat made me stop. When my eyes had adjusted to the
glare I saw another restaurant nearby with a notice, 'Other
Ranks Only'. As I stood hesitating, the proprietor, a stout, oily-

looking Egyptian, came out from the murky interior.

'You have friend? You know small officer? Not allowed in here. Took off ranks.' He pointed to the pips on my shoulders.

I peered past him. There were no patrons that I could see.

'Do you know where he went?'

He pointed to the back of the restaurant. 'In Gents over there with – '

I didn't wait for him to finish. When I opened the door there were three figures at the urinal, two of them military policemen. In the middle was Andy, looking pathetically small and defenceless between these burly men.

I waited respectfully for them to finish. Soon the MPs stood back, doing up their flies.

One of them said to Andy, 'Come on, Sir, you must be finished by now!'

'Be quiet, Sergeant, can't you see I'm concentrating?'

'Sir – '

'What's the trouble, Sergeant?' I asked. 'I'm with this officer.'

'Are you, Sir? Well, we've taken him in charge. First, he's acting under a false identity – this is an ORs' bar and he's taken off his badges of rank. Second, he's drunk.'

I beckoned the man out and explained the situation.

'I've got to get him back by six o'clock. I'm responsible for him, and he mustn't miss his treatment. Could you overlook it this time and leave it to me?'

'Very well, Sir, but don't let him drink any more.' He moved off with his companion.

Andy emerged looking fairly calm and sober. 'Those twits,' he said, 'how could I get tight on one bottle of beer!'

'Well, it's the Canadian stuff, very strong. You're not supposed to have any hooch at all.'

'I know. That's why I enjoyed it so much.'

I saw clearly now why the Major had said no alcohol. He wasn't drunk, but the mixture of beer and medication created a very fair imitation. To my relief the effects had worn off when I delivered him back to the hospital.

I wondered what would become of Andy after the war. I knew he was married; the photos showed a lovely young wife. Would he ever be fully cured, or able to hold down a job?

Would his record pursue him until he died? In a way he had given more than most people to his country through his invisible wounds.

For a while after seeing Andy I was weighed down by a leaden hopelessness. The loss of a friend through death is traumatic, but because of its finality one recovers. Watching the disintegration of a friend is worse. Andy was alive, existed still as a human shell even though the real Andy was gone. Despite hope, that most deceitful of all the virtues, the likelihood of his recovering his old self was too remote to have any reality. His condition was a lingering death.

A few months later I heard that he was indeed dead. It seemed to me best like that. Bright lights should go out suddenly, not smoulder ignominiously on.

My depression was compounded by a wound which refused to heal. Life had gone flat. Nothing seemed amusing or interesting; even people bored me. The static, touch-line atmosphere of base increased my sense of futility. Convalescent soldiers were only birds of passage to the depot staff, who went about their own business unmoved by our presence.

Boredom is one of the most miserable of human conditions. Sheltered here in this isolated depot there was too little to do and too much time to think. Housman put it perfectly:

> But men at times are sober
> And think by fits and starts.
> And if they think, they fasten
> Their hands upon their hearts.

And *if* they think ... impossible not to, alas.

Despite the surrender of the Germans in Tunisia the war wasn't over yet. There would be more fighting for us somewhere, sometime. The hardest thing to offset in action is suspense, which eats into your being. When in battle I tried to put a buffer between me and my fears. It took the form of a sort of mystical resignation. My buffer, I knew, was wearing a bit thin now, and experience made things harder instead of easier.

Lonely people become introspective. I tried to analyse my feelings in a diary. The entry for 6 July 1943 reads:

I'm like one of those starved little date palms one finds in the desert sometimes, all alone, complete bachelors, pining for water and cool breezes, and probably thinking all the time, 'If only I had another little date palm beside me, or could uproot myself and go over to Mersa Matruh and see what sort of trees my friends have grown into, friends I knew when we were little dates together!'

This evidently heralded a break-out from despondency, for the next day I went to see the MO, demanding that something be done about my leg.

'We're doing our best for you, you know,' he replied tartly, and prescribed a course of infra-red treatment.

'But I had that when I came here four weeks ago. It didn't do me any good.'

'Nothing seems to do you any good – we've tried everything. I suggest you take a week's leave, relax and enjoy yourself. Maybe that will help. It won't do you any harm anyway, and we can start the infra-red when you get back.'

Benito Finito

Cairo again. It was a quiet leave this time. The MO at base kept me under observation and insisted that I take things easy. I enjoyed the comparative peace and the companionship of men of my own corps.

News came through that we had successfully invaded Sicily, and then of the fall of Benito Mussolini. Now at last there was evidence that the war must be reaching its conclusion. Not only had the Axis armies been destroyed in North Africa, but the Allies were on European soil, and one of the dictators had been removed. We heard, too, of the bombing of Hamburg. How much longer could the enemy hold out against these blows?

This insidious question brought thoughts about my personal future. Some days I felt a faith that could move mountains and cleave the seas. On others I felt helpless, bullied by fate, too small, too insignificant to cope with the mighty train of circumstances that had started rolling in 1939.

These extremes of mood were intensified when I was recalled from leave and handed an urgent signal from battalion requiring me to return and take on the job of adjutant without delay.

Here indeed was a baffling complaint. As the junior captain in the battalion I had no pretensions towards such a promotion, nor, after my brief experience of paperwork at brigade, had I any ambitions in that direction.

Derby Day in the Desert

Battalion was now at Homs, about sixty miles east of Tripoli, on the coast. Settling down was confused by many contradictory feelings. The basic emotion was happiness. People matter so much more than places; because of friends I was often happy in the desert, and because of lack of them unhappy in the delta, or even in England.

I still retained my 'interesting' limp. Mac thought I should have waited a bit longer before returning: 'What good are you – just a potential casualty!' The CO, David Silvertop, eyed me with what seemed like less than enthusiasm: 'Hm. You can start by learning the ropes, and if your leg gets no better you'll have to go back to the delta.'

This was all rather discouraging, but the novelty of being back with the battalion and the concentration required in mastering my new job took my mind off the wound.

There were other distractions, as is always the case when a unit is out of battle and something like peace-time conditions obtain. One of these was a race-meeting organized by brigade, well advertised among all ranks, for which a most elaborate sweepstake had been arranged. So one sultry afternoon we motored out into the desert to the 'course'. The ochre-coloured ground was featureless and flat, stretching endlessly away into the heat haze. I met many friends from other units, including Oliver Wentworth-Stanley of the 11th Hussars, later godfather to my elder son.

A bugle-call signalled the opening ceremony. The brigade was drawn up on three sides of a square, faced on the open side by the Brigadier and his staff. After a few introductory remarks he turned to the drum from which the sweep tickets were to be drawn. The Brigade-Major rotated it, saluted, and asked the Brigadier to draw the first ticket.

With ostentatious nonchalance he plunged his hand into the aperture, averting his eyes in the general direction of heaven. After a long grope he extracted a ticket and passed it to the Brigade-Major. A deep hush fell on the attendant troops.

'I wonder who's the lucky chap!' he spluttered, grinning fatuously. 'Well, come on, man!' he urged, as the Brigade-Major, pink and wooden, handed him the winning ticket.

'Wait for it, wait for it!' the Brigadier cried. 'Who can it be!

One hundred pounds goes to the lucky – er – Oh my God – it's me!'

Silence continued to grip the ranks.

'Well, er, now, second prize, sixty pounds, what!'

The drum was rotated again, and again the Brigadier drew out a ticket.

'This time it goes to – goes to – ah – Major, er, the Brigade-Major ... '

The silence in the ranks was tangible.

Of the tickets drawn the first ten went to officers. Fate sometimes moves in a mysterious way. The soldiers, however, did not interpret it as fate.

Shortly after this embarrassing débâcle the races began. The jockeys were local Arabs in full regalia, a magnificent sight with their turbans and robes flying in the wind. Betting was very difficult as the sheiks had 'fixed' every race according to some mysterious hierarchical custom. The riders got so excited that with fiendish yells they continued flat out past the winning-post and raced for miles into the pink hazy distances of the desert, the MPs chasing them in jeeps to bring back the winner for his prize.

At first I found the job of adjutant daunting. I had no enthusiasm for it, and one cannot do justice to boring work. My role swung between that of office-boy and diplomat. I discovered that the only way to ensure things were done was to be a nuisance to everyone, which did not suit my pleasure-loving nature.

Gradually, however, I began to see beyond the tedious routine and the forest of papers daily planted on my desk. No longer did I fear making some frightful blunder leading to ignominious demotion. The CO was more tolerant than his manner suggested. He had received the training and expertise that goes into the education of a regular officer in peace-time, and was sensitive to my position, that of a temporary soldier thrown into a responsible job on which depended the welfare of so many men. To me military law, disciplinary matters and the archaic etiquette remained an impenetrable mystery because I was incapable of appreciating all their relevance.

The strangest cult was entitled Man Management, which suggested that there was some norm by which all men could

be ruled, from which individuality was an unspeakable deviation. This seemed the sort of training course a zoo-keeper might
undergo: Monkey Management, perhaps, or How to Handle
Hippopotami. In my heretical innocence, born of a few years'
teaching before the war, I had believed that leadership was
something instinctive rather than acquired; but the army recognized in its wisdom that in all activities there must be a minimum standard, and that not all officers can achieve a valuable
rapport with their men without a basic training.

What I found most rewarding was dealing with the men's
problems; discussing the marriage crises, which were exacerbated by delays in communication and the absence of personal
contact between man and wife; attempting to console over the
deaths of relatives; recommending compassionate leave when
possible; even handling complaints which varied from the
irrelevant to the flippant or downright half-witted. In short, I
revelled in being a military nanny.

My chief ally was Paddy, the Quartermaster, a long-service
regular. He was the archetypal Irishman, massive, with a face
like a ripe apple in shape and colour, small turned-up nose,
thick black eyebrows, and laughing blue eyes. These sparkled
when I reminded him of the stinking greatcoat from a decom-
posing corpse he had supplied me with at Alamein.

'Jaysus, aren't you the fussy man!'

I began to enjoy organizing other people's lives, coming to
believe I had the squadron leaders under my thumb. To my
surprise I even relished official correspondence, though David
returned some of my effusions unsigned as being too flippant.

All this time my leg refused to heal. It wasn't painful but it
reduced my mobility, so I couldn't take any exercise. Lack of
fitness does not lead to efficiency. At last, in desperation, I
asked Mac how long he thought it would take to heal.

'Don't know. Friend of mine got hit in the leg two years ago
and he's still in bandages.'

'Be serious, Mac.'

'I am. You've no idea how inebriated you look with that
limp. Scotch?'

Back to Blighty
A month later we were camped outside Alexandria awaiting

embarkation. We didn't know it then, but we were returning to Blighty to be fattened up for D-Day.

The logistical work of putting a whole battalion onto a ship was grinding and infuriating. When everything seemed to be completed something would happen to necessitate a complicated rearrangement. After taking a few well-earned days of leave in Cairo the CO returned in a tetchy mood, disapproving of all my plans and saying so in direct speech.

At last, however, final orders came through, rather late in the evening. Embarkation would start at 0600 hours next day. At 0330 hours the CO woke me, asking if everything was ready. I said yes, there was nothing that could usefully be done now.

'What the bloody hell do you mean!' he bawled, waking half the camp and causing me to leap out of bed so violently that my wounded leg reminded me painfully of its presence.

'Get up, you [unrepeatable] and do a tour of the area. See every squadron leader and make sure they know exactly what they have to do.'

There was an extraordinary unanimity in the replies of the squadron leaders when I woke them. In each case it amounted to 'Bugger off', or words to that effect.

At dawn we boarded lighters and were ferried out to our ship. On the way we were overtaken by a speedboat racing towards the liner nearest to us. Standing in the bows of the launch, swaying rather more than the motion of the sea warranted, was a middle-aged Merchant Navy officer clasping the gunwales. A rope-ladder was thrown over the stern of the liner. He tried to catch hold of it, missed, and descended like a wounded bird into the sea. The launch made a quick circle; the crew hauled him aboard, shook him violently, and edged the craft slowly up to the dangling ladder. We held our breath in horror, believing we were witnessing a tragedy. As we sailed closer we were astonished to see the crew rolling about with laughter. One of them cupped his hands and yelled to an officer on the deck above, 'He's sobered up enough to have another go!'

This time the officer clung to the ladder while it was hauled cautiously up from above. This exhibition of nautical know-how gave us great confidence for the remainder of our voyage.

The convoy, a double line of assorted ships, stretched ahead as far as we could see. Our destination was a Dutch luxury ship of the same line as the famous *Niewe Amsterdam*. Such a contrast in conditions would be hard to imagine; from desert to deck, from bivvy to bunk.

In the afternoon the ships started to move forward, exact in formation, a great armada suggesting sea power, yet defenceless. In our ignorance of nautical matters we began to wonder what our fate would be if the enemy attacked with submarines or aircraft. Then someone pointed towards the west. Out from a bank of mist a flotilla of destroyers was steaming purposefully towards us. Driving straight in our direction with what seemed reckless speed, they put their helms down to port at the last moment, forming up in line ahead parallel to the convoy; some continuing along to accompany the leading ships, others slowing down to accommodate themselves to our pace.

One destroyer made straight towards us. It appeared to have misjudged the speed and distance; but, having been brought up on the invincibility and efficiency of the Royal Navy, we assumed that the commander knew exactly, to a hair's breadth, what he was doing. As the ship swerved to port, heeling to starboard on account of its speed, the young commander standing at attention on his little bridge, saluting our captain, it became evident that our basest hopes were about to be fulfilled.

The impact was severe enough for the naval officer to fall flat on his face as the destroyer bounced off us, taking one of the protective wooden fenders from our side. It lost impetus and was quickly put into reverse. The young commander staggered to his feet, saluted, and called out to our captain, 'I say, Sir, I'm frightfully sorry!'

The latter was now leaning over the port railing of his bridge, a large blond man, florid, bristling with indignation and rage. He spoke in Dutch, but the drift was clear. His tirade lasted several minutes, during which the destroyer commander remained at the salute, trying to maintain a dignified balance as his little ship rolled in the waves caused by our accelerating progress.

As soon as we were aboard Mac decided that I should be consigned to the ship's hospital in the hope that some treatment might heal my leg. I was the only patient in the ward.

Next day the CO came to see me.

'I've some news for you. You know Pete Pyman is now chief of staff of 30 Corps? He's sent a signal that he wants you to be seconded as his personal assistant. I take it you'd like that? Good. This means you'll be leaving the battalion, so we'll need a new adjutant. I've decided to appoint Jock Balharrie. He's a regular, so it will be good for his career. Would you mind if he took over right away – you can't very well do the job from down here!'

'Of course not, Sir. Jock will be first class.' I felt both over-whelmed and relieved. 'Sir, what happens at Corps HQ? I've no idea of the set-up.'

'Quite a lot! Pete is in charge of planning, I believe. You'll be pretty busy!'

When he left I was visited by the medical officer in charge of the hospital, a wing commander. He examined my wound and left orders with a very pretty nursing sister, aptly named Felicity, that I was to have my leg raised above hip level and to lie on my back with a minimum of movement. No visitors, no alcohol. He smiled kindly, giving me the impression of a rather quiet man who would expect discipline without the necessity of having to enforce it.

That evening several officers from the battalion came to see me. The first was carrying two bottles of beer.

'Your ration,' he said, handing me one of them. 'I drew it for you as you couldn't get it yourself.'

'Damn nice of you,' I said. 'Look, there are some glasses over there. Cheers!'

At that moment Jock came in. He was carrying two bottles of beer.

'Your ration,' he said, handing me one of them. 'I drew it for you as you couldn't get it yourself.'

'Damn nice of you,' I said. 'Look ... '

Thoughtfully, every officer had drawn a bottle for me. When a dozen or more had arrived we settled down to a splen-did party. It was at its height when Felicity rushed in.

'The MO's doing his rounds,' she said breathlessly, looking with horror at the empties, and at me sitting on the edge of my bed. 'For goodness' sake hide those bottles – and you people, get out, quick!'

SEVEN

Planning for D-Day

I was married on 18 December 1943. Our brief honeymoon was interrupted by my admittance to hospital on Christmas Eve suffering from pneumonia.

On emerging I appeared before a medical board and was asked how much sick leave I thought I was entitled to before returning to duty.

'A week, perhaps?' I asked, 'or would that be too much?' The MO nodded before filling in a form which he handed to me.

'A week? I think it wouldn't do you any harm to complete your honeymoon – I've recommended twenty-eight days.'

I spent these in a little hotel at Shefford, a village near Hitchin in Bedfordshire. My wife, Paddy, who was in the WAAF, was stationed nearby and spent her off-duty times with me. It was a period of near-peace and happiness, the wonderment at my new estate tempered by apprehension about the future.

At that time, with the great battles in North Africa over, the Italian campaign in stalemate, and the Russians urging the Allies into action, the war seemed static. The opening of a Second Front occupied every mind. But when? And where? Norway? The Pas de Calais? If we could draw off some of the German divisions from the Russian Front the war would be over more quickly, and people complained that it was typical of the Top Brass to be doing nothing about it.

On completion of my sick leave I joined Pete at 30 Corps HQ at Newmarket. As he briefed me about my job I began to understand the complexity of shipping a vast army across the Channel into enemy-held territory. Detailed planning was complicated by the fact that the amount of shipping space changed daily according to the needs of the Royal and US Navies in the Pacific, so that allocations made today would have to be amended tomorrow. The intensity of work reduced several very competent officers to nervous breakdowns.

Secrecy was imperative, and it says much for the integrity and discipline of the thousands of people in the know that the invasion caught the Germans napping – remarkably, given the dangers of possible indiscretion or the activities of enemy spies. Every senior officer had a map of the target area, and these maps had to be concealed from unofficial eyes. The date was not yet fixed but the intention was to attack in early summer. It was almost unbearable to know all these matters and never refer to them, even indirectly, to outsiders. When we went to relax in a pub it was inevitable that some civilian would come up and ask where the Second Front would be, and when. The alternatives were to pretend total ignorance, or invent something, like, 'Don't know, old man. Norway seems likely, or Greece.' I preferred the first option.

Towards the end of our time at Newmarket, planning staff were given a week's leave, phased so that all would be present during the final six weeks leading up to D-Day. Paddy, now stationed at Mildenhall, tried to get leave to coincide with mine, but she was being sent on a course and her Commanding Officer refused permission. Conscious that I might never see her again I decided to take action.

The officer commanding RAF Mildenhall, dubbed 'Square', was from Down Under, and had the reputation of being a brilliant commander whose relations with his subordinates were more informal than those adopted by British officers. Aware that I might be making a complete fool of myself, but driven by desperation, I borrowed a jeep and set out to see him.

That night there was a low cloud ceiling, so the bombers were grounded, which was lucky for me. I went straight to the guardroom, where a courteous aircraftman rang the Station Commander, then followed a small truck containing an armed guard to a house set back in a garden. The door was opened by a short man who seemed as broad as he was tall. He invited me in and I started to tell him my story.

'Wait a moment,' he said, 'I see you have the fighting man's ribbon.' He looked more closely. 'Yes, and the Africa Star, Eighth Army clasp. Let's have a drink.'

He opened a cupboard and took out a bottle of Scotch. 'Go

on,' he said. When I had finished he nodded. 'I see your problem. Yes, yes, I know why you must have your leave now. I'll ring the Queen Bee.'

He picked up the phone. When he'd explained the situation I could hear a strident female voice which did not seem at all in sympathy with his request. After listening for a while he gave me an outrageous wink and put his hand over the mouthpiece: 'I'm going to have to fix her!' Then, into the mouthpiece, 'This is an order – LACW Ross will be given a week's leave starting at 0800 hours next Thursday. Is that clear?' A pause, then a strangled 'Yes, Sir.'

'Good. I've been longing to have a crack at her – a very bossy lady. Your glass.'

We chatted for an hour or two, during which we covered many subjects and emptied many glasses.

'My wife's away,' he said. 'I'm glad you looked in, I was getting a bit bored. One for the road!'

We staggered out and I clambered into my jeep. 'Square' walked the twenty or thirty yards to the gate, shining a small torch to guide me. Having no lights except the little slits in the headlamp covers, I drove straight towards him. The drive seemed a bit bumpy. Climbing out to thank him I received a sharp scratch in my right calf.

'My God, I've driven over the roses!'

'Have you? Bad show. I'll get some men to straighten them out before the wife gets back. She rather fancies them. The roses, I mean. Good luck!'

For the final phases of planning Corps HQ was moved from Newmarket to London. Our offices were in the pleasant square off Victoria Street in which stands Westminster Cathedral.

Pete's office was on the first floor. Opposite the windows was a huge map of Normandy stretching from wall to wall, always kept shuttered. When it was needed the first job was to close the windows, since it was visible from the street, and then to get the keys from the senior Staff Officer.

Many conferences took place in this room. I sat at a desk set back from the table round which the Top Brass sat, and took notes for Pete. On one occasion there was a clash between General Bucknall, the Corps Commander, and Major-General Sir Miles Graham, commanding the 50th Highland Division. The infantry had been issued with a new type of bayonet, shorter and lighter than the ones used since 1914. General Graham said his men preferred the old bayonet, which they were used to handling and in which they had confidence. The Corps Commander, not known for his flexibility of mind, demurred, pointing out that the new bayonet was already distributed and that to change now would create an unnecessary complication at a stage when administration was stretched to its limit.

Pete intervened with his usual diplomacy. Morale, he said, was very important, especially with troops who would be in the first wave of the assault on the beaches. But, as the Corps Commander had remarked, time was short. He referred the matter to George Webb, that splendid buccaneer, who winked in my direction and said, 'Peter, take a note that the 50th Division will receive their old bayonets back again on Monday!'

Nothing could be more calculated to annoy the Corps Commander. To him junior officers should be like Victorian children, seen (if their presence were unavoidable) and not heard. George's addressing me by my Christian name was very bad form, more especially in this instance because his banter-ing tone implied a rebuke for the Corps Commander.

George had arrived a few minutes late for this meeting. As he passed my desk he stopped, stared at me, and said, 'I saw you last night, you filthy beast! Surprised you're able to be about today!'

'Sir,' I replied with mock dignity, 'I did not go out last night and I went to bed very early!'

'Spare me the disgusting details!' he said, and swept on to his place at the table. Throughout this exchange the Corps Commander wore an expression of grim disapproval.

As Pete's personal assistant I often drove his staff car. This sounds a pleasant occupation, but the fact that all signposts had been removed from the roads often meant study of maps before setting out and quick thinking at awkward forks and crossroads. A few days before D-Day I drove him to Swanage in Dorset, where we were to stay while observing a full-scale landing exercise nearby.

'Do you know the way, Peter?'

'Yes, Sir, very well, I used to live in Swanage before the war and we often drove up to London and back.'

'Good. Whatever you do, avoid Bournemouth. I don't want any delays.'

Somehow the country looked different now. I followed the main road successfully as far as Ringwood. Pete, immersed in some papers, looked up and asked me where we were.

'Not far now, Sir. We're about thirty miles from Wareham.'

'Really? Seems to me we're in the outskirts of Bournemouth.'

Hastily I halted the car and got out my map.

'Er – yes, Sir. I'm afraid you're right, Sir. Sorry.'

'I should damned well think so. Find the right road and put your foot down. I've got to meet the Corps Commander in Swanage at six o'clock!'

For the rest of the journey there was a tangible atmosphere of *froideur*.

The exercise took place at Studland Bay across a stretch of shore chosen for its likeness to some Normandy beaches, with cliffs as well as sand. The Top Brass, accompanied by their underlings, stood in an imposing group at the top of the most southerly cliff, the best vantage-point from which to view every phase of this dress rehearsal. Its importance was stressed by the fact that the highest-ranked officers of every arm were there, among them the Commander-in-Chief of all British forces, His Majesty King George VI.

Live ammunition was to be used. First there was to be a naval bombardment, the target being imaginary fortifications some miles inland. Then, giving close support to the landing troops, came a wave of Whitley bombers. Beside me was Michael, ADC to one of the generals. The bombers approached like menacing birds.

'Get down quick!' yelled Michael above the noise, flinging himself down on the grass.

'Why? We're not the target – '

'Look at those RAF officers, you fool!'

I looked. Of the group of senior officers outlined on the edge of the cliff only those in army and navy uniforms were standing, shading their eyes as they watched the planes sweep overhead. All the RAF officers were flat on their faces.

As I got to my feet Michael was laughing.

'*They're* not taking any risks! They know their own chaps too well!'

The planes rumbled on inland and in a few moments we saw the bombs tumbling downward. To my horror I realized that the target area was on the golf-course, where I'd spent many happy hours before the war. It did occur to me that the craters might later be used to make a few extra bunkers, but that was small comfort; one hates to see an old friend being ravaged. By now the first of the sea-borne troops were rushing across the beach and scrambling up into the bracken, spraying the ground ahead with machine-gun fire. I didn't see any generals ducking down, nor had the admirals gone to ground during the naval bombardment. But the margin of error is greater when you are flying at hundreds of miles an hour. A misjudgment of a second means delivering your bomb on the wrong spot by several miles.

As Michael summed it up, 'They're not really windy, but they know their onions – if you see what I mean!'

D-Day, 6 June 1944

This day will be remembered for as long as human records are kept. After five years of war, most of them on the losing side, the greatest sea-borne army in the history of the world began its landings in Normandy. The great aggressor, the Nazi wolf, could now see its intended victims approaching the lair.

Fortunately I had no command that day, because I woke up with raging toothache, which is the ultimate in egotism, in that no thought or feeling can be projected beyond that throbbing centre of pain.

After a hurried glance at the map in the Operations Room, where I noted with distant unreality that in some sectors landings had successfully taken place, I went to find Pete. He looked up from his breakfast, his usual confidence embellished by a smile.

'Splendid start! What did you say?'

'Toothache, Sir.'

'I see.' His expression turned to one of knowing contempt, as if I had invented the toothache in order to avoid the landing. 'We go aboard at 1300 hours. I shall need you as soon as possible. Better see a dentist at once.' He dismissed me with an impatient flick of the hand and turned back to his breakfast.

I commandeered a jeep and drove to the Army Dental

Centre at Cosham, near Portsmouth, a little way from our HQ. On the way excited people going to work shouted at me, 'It's started – the Second Front!' I responded with a regal wave of the hand.

The dentist replaced an enormous stopping which had come out, and I returned hastily to HQ, where Pete received me with a forgiving smile.

General Bucknall, his ADC, Claud Hastings, Pete and I boarded a destroyer. As we started out into the Solent I was overwhelmed by the sight of so many ships, large and small, assembled in so small a channel. How had the enemy not spotted this huge and closely packed armada and sent across a fleet of bombers to destroy it?

Steaming into the Channel we entered a laneway between the rows of shipping stretching endlessly southward, vessels of all descriptions, from battleships to tugs, destroyers to landing craft, some heading for France, others returning. Each kept station exactly behind the ship in front, the spaces even in length between them.

We sped along, alone in this great company, faster than the flanking convoys. The Corps Commander and Pete retired to the Captain's cabin. Claud and I watched the radar screen, something we had never seen before, while the Navigation Officer explained its symbols to us.

On this voyage I came as near to knowing Claud as was possible. I respected him greatly because he had fought with distinction in the First World War and so was at an age when he could – and should – have been employed in some adminis-trative post in England. He came of an old family in the south of Ireland and had been General Bucknall's closest friend for many years, Bucknall appointing him his ADC when he became a general.

Claud was a splendid anachronism. Tall, upright, balding, with laughter-lines at the corners of his eyes, he wore a mono-cle and used a long ebony and silver cigarette-holder. The product of a society now moribund, to him, respect for the decencies, for integrity and good manners, was the norm. He would never fail to change for dinner, whatever the circum-stances, even if alone: not a mere pandering to convention but an expression of self-discipline. He watched the radar screen with a mixture of interest and distaste.

When the Navy Signals Officer told us we were almost in sight of land we went on deck. It was twilight. Against a pale sky we saw a long black cloud stretching over the coast, caused by the battles that had raged since dawn.

We went aboard HMS *Bulolo*, the command ship, as darkness closed in. She was lying a mile off shore. A huge relief map showed that the landings had, in the main, gone according to plan, and bridgeheads several miles deep had been established, though the Americans had met determined resistance and suffered heavy casualties before achieving their objectives.

30 Corps had landed on Gold Beach. After consultations with higher command Bucknall and Pete prepared to go ashore. The sea was now so choppy that the landing craft sent to transport us found it hard to stay alongside, and the tumultuous waves made it impossible to climb down the ladder on *Bulolo*'s side and step aboard. To my horror a large net was spread across the little craft so that we could jump down.

First went the Corps Commander, who projected himself rather ungracefully, his outstretched arms like the wings of a skinny bird. The crew hastily gathered him in – a net in a boat tossed by a rough sea is not the easiest surface to manoeuvre on – to restore some of the dignity he had surrendered in the cause of his country. Pete followed, his eyes shut as he took off, possibly in prayer. Certainly his aim was faultless; he landed in a tight ball clutching his crotch. Claud took off his monocle and put his cigarette-holder in his pocket. He drew himself up, muttered something about being the last of his line, and dived head first into the middle of the net.

I watched intently, noting the possible consequences. If I jumped too short or too far I would strike a bulwark and be killed or maimed for life. Was it better to jump as the craft rose on a wave, or as it descended? From the depth of the craft's dark interior Claud's voice penetrated my frozen mind: 'Jump, you bloody clot, it's quite painless!' I forced myself to take his advice. The sensation of flying released my tension, as did the moment of astonishment when I landed and realized I was still alive.

We discovered that we were aboard an American L/C, which accounted, perhaps, for the somewhat informal manner of our

arrival. Even the Corps Commander, no believer in informality, nodded amiably when a rating asked him, 'Say, do those
red labels mean you're a *real* general?'

We had a bumpy ride ashore as the blunt bow of the L/C
battered against the waves. Forty yards from the beach we saw
that we were heading towards a red light. Someone with a
loud hailer yelled, 'Get back! Mines! Mines everywhere – get
back!' It was fortunate that our commander, who seemed
unaware that red means danger, had earlier warped his craft
with a kedge. The hawser was slowly drawn in until we were
well clear of land. We headed east and soon saw a green light
inviting us in.

Once ashore Pete and Bucknall went off to HQ in a jeep,
leaving Claud and me to assemble their baggage. There was
tremendous activity on the beach as more and more senior
officers arrived. Men were moving equipment towards the
dunes, and wounded were carried down and put aboard craft
returning to England. Every now and again a resonant roar
above us declared that a sixteen-pound shell from one of our
warships was beginning its twenty-mile journey inland.

Suddenly the whole area was illuminated by silver flares,
blinding us for a moment as they shattered the darkness. Then
followed the rattle of machine-gun and cannon fire. As I looked
around bewildered for our assailants, a hail of bullets spattered
the sand from enemy aircraft sweeping low over the beach, the
trace of their bullets adding an ironic beauty to the scene.

With a frenzied leap I dived into a slit trench. A large soldier
was lying near the end. 'Move up!' I shouted through the din,
pushing him with my shoulder. There was no reply. Obviously
he had been dead since morning.

Hearing a familiar voice I looked up. It was Claud, monocle
glinting in the flickering lights, his left hand on his hip, his
right brandishing the cigarette-holder.

'That's right, Ross,' he drawled, 'make yourself at home.
Don't mind me. I just love standing here being shot at!'

'Claud, there's no room – ' I started, but ducked as another
plane discharged its cannon overhead. When I looked up again
Claud was strolling across the beach towards the jeep, which
had been sent back to collect us. I ran after him and helped him
to load the baggage, then we set off for the village of Le Hamel.

After so many years of war it was a strange sensation to be on French soil. The Nazi Occupation was so complete, so firmly established, that the whole concept of life in France had been unreal. We had been far afield, wrapped up in our own problems, in North Africa, or Italy, or elsewhere. Trying to imagine life in France, without adequate information, was like trying to imagine life on some planet far away; we could only feel sorrow at the humiliation of the people.

The landings and events on subsequent days have been described by countless military historians, in memoirs by senior officers, journalists, novelists and poets. My own memories are disordered but vivid. First among them is the sight and stench of dead horses, their stomachs grotesquely distended, lying in the ditches and fields. To a greater extent than any other army, except possibly the Russian, the *Wehrmacht* saved fuel by using horse transport. In any battle these animals suffered heavy casualties, and one only hoped that someone had the compassion, and the means, to put them out of their agony.

On D+1 Pete sent me to a farm near Le Hamel to tell the owners to bury the carcases. As I walked up the straight narrow little path the farmer's wife appeared at the door. She was a thin-faced, dark woman, and I felt uncomfortable as she eyed me with distrust. I explained why I had come. She made no answer. Thinking she might not have understood my French, I said it again.

Looking at me with contempt she said, 'Who do you think will do that? I am alone. My husband was killed by the Germans, and my son was killed by one of your bombs. He was fifteen. The hands have all gone. And now the horses are dead, so I cannot even work the farm.'

She stopped talking, but continued to stare at me. Tears came into her eyes. She pressed her lips together and held herself erect as though determined not to give in to her despair in front of me. I realized the atrocious insensitivity of what I had ordered her to do.

'Madame,' I said heavily, 'I am deeply sorry. We'll send some soldiers to bury the horses.'

Next morning Pete told me to reconnoitre the road leading west from Bayeux, which was not far from HQ. I went in a

little tracked vehicle known as a 'Weasel', a kind of baby brother
to the Bren carrier. We were intrigued that the signposts had
not been removed, as in England. Fortunately a glance at my
map showed that they were pointed in the wrong directions,
just in time to save my driving straight into enemy territory.

We cautiously left the road and drove slowly onto green
downs above some cliffs. I was thinking how like the South
Downs they looked when a group of about twenty German
soldiers emerged from behind a hedge. There was no possi-
bility of covering them all with a gun and I thought my last
moment had come. They ran towards us, their hands raised in
surrender, crying, 'Take us prisoner, please!' They were elderly
men, slow-moving, clearly a section of the low-quality troops
used in a static role on parts of the 'Atlantic Wall'.

'OK,' I said, pointing to the road, 'take that road eastwards.
We'll follow you.'

'Nein, nein!' they expostulated in shocked voices, 'we're
sick, all got stomach-trouble, cannot march. You give us ride!'

'How do you think you'd all fit on this?' I asked, laughing.
'Now, start walking, there's no hurry, and it's only five miles!'

It was difficult to hate these pathetic creatures, whose presence in the forces revealed the desperation of the Germans in
making good their enormous losses. Later in the campaign we
were faced by children, hastily armed, untrained and terrified,
looking like pantomime clowns in uniforms far too big for
them.

One of the greatest tragedies of war is that most casualties
occur among the young, the brave, the intelligent, in short the
best, who must be in the thick of it, so that potential leaders,
political and military, are lost. The most dramatic example is
France, where casualties were so great in the 1914–18 war that
nearly a whole generation was wiped out, a generation which
should have provided the commanders in 1940. Instead we had
the spectacle of a great military nation led by pusillani-mous
old men who were happier to hide behind the Maginot Line
than go out and attack, and then the shameful collabora-tion
by poor old Pétain and the traitor Laval. Fortunately for France
there were still some fine soldiers left, men like de Gaulle,
Leclerc and Koenig, who, along with such resolute men of the
Resistance as Gaston Deferre, restored France to her former

glory.

One hot Sunday in July Pete sent me with a message to a forward unit. The tank-churned roads were dusty with a fine, disease-carrying dust which whitened the jeep and caked upon our sweating hands and faces. The rotting corpse smell was still in the air, although by now the battle had lumbered beyond this area. The ditches were no longer filled by the carcases of horses, and villagers had begun to tidy the rubble into heaps.

Bystanders glanced listlessly at us as we passed, showing small enthusiasm for their liberators. To them we were merely instruments of the havoc that had been wrought upon the fair and fruitful countryside of Normandy. The grand strategy of the Allies meant nothing to these people, whose homes had been ruined, families bereft, and means of livelihood destroyed. Yet in fact they had escaped the rougher edges of the war until their country was selected for the liberation of so many millions, for whom they did not care a sou.

The Normans are a sturdy, businesslike race, instinctively classifying sentiment and politics as a waste of time. Prosperity and dreaming make poor companions, so the Normans live in the present, farming their holdings with dogged skill, respectable and independent. The Germans, recognizing these qualities and also conscious of the necessity of a peaceful coastline, interfered as little as possible in their pursuits.

Because communications were poor in France during the Occupation, those that were open giving priority to troop movements and subject to continuous damage from the RAF, the Paris market was denied to the Normans. This would have been very serious, since dairy produce and apples could not in wartime conditions be stored for long, had not a substitute market been provided by the *Wehrmacht*. The soldiers treated the people with consideration and paid well for what they bought. Outrages such as had occurred in other parts of France were unheard of, and some Norman girls married German soldiers. There was little need for the Maquis to take overt action: martyrs are not bred of contentment. The Normans were prepared to pay lip-service to the Germans and profit from their trade, but they loved them no better than they loved us.

As the Allies' preparations for invasion neared completion, the Germans began to live on tenterhooks. The screen lifted and both populations, the occupied and the occupying, showed their feelings openly. An RAF pilot, shot down near Bayeux, was given a military funeral by the citizens. As a reprisal the Germans took into captivity all the pupils of a local school. Memories were not dim, either, of those men of Normandy who had been taken prisoners of war in 1940 and not yet returned to their families, some of them unheard of since.

On this bright morning, as we motored through the hedge-lined roads, and gazed lazily at the little fields and the orchards making formal patterns on the undulating grassland, I realized the lasting nature of land that is well looked after. Armies come and go leaving smashed farmsteads, trampled fields and outraged orchards, yet in a few months the spoor of their marching has almost disappeared.

We came round a bend into a village. We had to halt because the congregation was pouring out of the church, a slow, black stream of humanity, over the road and onto the green on our right. At last the priest appeared behind them. I was about to tell my driver to start up when I noticed that the people were not going home, but gathering on the green. They were laughing, shouting, nudging each other and lifting small children to see something that was going on in the centre of the crowd. Among them were some British soldiers, looking stonily embarrassed, as though they felt they were intruding, yet too interested to go away.

Leaving my driver to guard the jeep, I pushed my way into the crowd. In the middle a number of young men, some wearing Maquis brassards and all armed with Sten guns, surrounded an elderly woman seated on a stool. An eighteen-year-old boy was cutting off her hair.

At bay, helpless, the focus of hundreds of pairs of hostile eyes, she bore herself with a resigned, even a dignified, air, though it was plain that tears were very near the surface. Unlike the rest of the women, all dressed in their black Sunday hats and coats, she wore a brown, flowered cotton dress, and an apron. It looked as if she had been surprised while cooking lunch and her visitors had given her no option in the matter of her appearance. Obviously, for reasons soon to become clear, she had not been in church.

'What's it all about?' I asked a burly, red-faced farmer next to me.

'C'est une collaboratrice. On lui coupe les cheveux.'

'Why?'

He shrugged his shoulders. 'She merits it well. Ridicule is of all the punishments the most humiliating.'

I watched the barber, who was setting about his work with relish. All the time he was talking and muttering. A silence fell upon the people as he became carried away, so I could catch something of what he was saying.

'Nom de Dieu! That is for Jean, mon pauvre Jean, my brave brother! You bitch, you told them. And now he possesses not even a grave ... Eh bien! ... and that is some more for him!' Here a large handful of hair was half cut, half torn away. 'And this is for his comrades, André and Georges. Sit still, old cow, sit still – yes, still! as the American pilot you betrayed to the Boches is now still. Really, this is too good for you. Soon I shall have to use my razor, and then ... the temptation will be strong.

'We hate you, old woman, we despise you! Look about you. See all those people you know so well, who are laughing at you? Their laughter lacks joy, does it not? You betrayed them when it paid you – but now, now!' His voice rose, then dropped again as he went on in level tones. 'Do you expect us to believe that you were only pretending to help the Boches, that all the time you were on our side? Why did you give away so many, then? Death gives no change. Three men of this village, and the American aviator, are dead because of you. Was that all part of the game? High stakes, eh, Madame the Informer!

'And your son, prisoner in Germany since 1940 ... he will be home soon – perhaps. How proud he will be of his mother! He will look for his old pals, André, Georges and Jean, but he will not be able to find them. What will he do? He will ask you, his mother, where they are. And you, and only you, will be able to tell him.'

He worked now without speaking. Then, 'Ah! c'est fini, alors. Go now, old traitor, go to your home, and hold your head up high!'

Silently the crowd parted, and the old woman lurched slowly down the street to her cottage, her bald pate shining ridiculously in the sunlight. There was still no sound from the people. Then she took out her handkerchief to dry her eyes. The tension snapped, and suddenly laughter and mocking insults followed her. On she went, neither increasing nor slackening her pace, but rolling slightly from side to side in the desolation of her misery. Justice had been meted out to her in public, justice was filling her ears with harsh laughter, a sound that would live with her forever.

And her son, the prisoner of war, was it not possible that by making some bargain she had stood between him and his torturers? Or between him and his murderers? Had she perhaps betrayed her village for his sake? He was all she had.

In any administrative organization, be it a city office or a mobile military unit, a routine must be followed. So, despite the battles raging all round us, the constant expectation of attack from the air or long-range artillery, work continued at Corps Main and Tac HQs as normally as possible. Duty officers sat up all night keeping in touch with units engaged in battle, recording every message in the log. Next day these were acted upon by senior staff officers, information was collated and given to the Chief of Staff, who discussed it with the General Commanding so that he could make his decisions. Conferences were convened, visits made to units, indents completed by the Quartermaster's staff for supplies, and provisions sent forward. Command could be carried out only if there were controlled efficiency at staff level, and this had to be maintained whatever the battle situation.

One day I arrived back at HQ, then in a field a mile southeast of Bayeux, as lunch was being served. There was only one vacant seat, beside a visiting general who wore the insignia of the Airborne Forces. This was Sir Frederick 'Boy' Browning, husband of Daphne du Maurier. The Corps Commander, General Bucknall, was at the head of the table, with 'Boy' on his left. He was a charming man with a superb intellect, who most courteously gave me a great deal of his attention, even though we were both sitting so close to the Corps Commander. I referred to Tolstoy's *War and Peace*, then my knapsack book, which I found fascinating for two reasons. First, the curse of

Napoleon's invasion of Russia had parallels with the current
German invasion: the same place-names were mentioned and
the immediate objective, Moscow, was in danger once more of
being captured. Second, Tolstoy's analysis of the part played
by leaders in war and peace was of particular interest when
applied to contemporary figures – Churchill, Hitler, Eisenhower,
Montgomery and others.

I asked 'Boy' Browning if he agreed with Tolstoy's thesis
that what historians call great men do not shape events, but are
rather thrown up by those events. Tolstoy described Napoleon
as 'a man without convictions, without habits, without
traditions, without a name, and not even a Frenchman, [who]
emerges – by what seems the strangest chances – from among
all the seething French parties, and, without joining any one of
them, is borne forward to a prominent position'.

'Boy' smiled and said he did agree.

'Consider Churchill. If there had been no Second World War
he would have been classified by historians as a controversial
First Sea Lord in World War I, a cantankerous parliamentarian,
a brilliant but ultimately unfulfilled man.'

'That sums it up perfectly, Sir,' I replied. 'Tolstoy refers to
rulers and generals as history's slaves – '

This was too much for the Corps Commander.

'I think we've more important things to discuss,' he cut in
icily, eyeing me with crushing distaste.

It seemed as much a rebuke to 'Boy' as to me. Like all
people who reach a position higher than their talents warrant,
Bucknall shied away from any views that might undermine his
small con-fidence. In fact there was no more conversation at all
during that meal, but an upstart captain had been satisfactorily
shot down.

At the beginning of August plans were completed for 30
Corps to break out southwards, capturing Villers Bocage and
Aunay-sur-Odon, in order to protect the left flank of the
American V Corps. To stress the necessity for speed, Monty
had said that he wanted Villers Bocage 'for breakfast'.

Pete and I set out at once to find the Corps Commander,
who was visiting forward formations, but had not acknowledged signals about the planned attack. On the way Pete
confided to me his anxiety that Bucknall did not understand

the urgency of the situation.

When finally contact was made and Pete had explained Monty's plan, Bucknall instructed General Erskine, commanding 7 Armoured Division (the original 'Desert Rats') to change their axis and move immediately against the German positions at Villers Bocage. Despite every effort, this operation could not be carried out swiftly because of the narrowness of the roads, the proximity of the hedges making it impossible for a tank to turn, or even sometimes to traverse its gun. When at length they reached Villers Bocage they could make no progress against the German screen. Infantry were needed, but Bucknall had preferred to land 7 Armoured Division before his infantry, and so there were none available.

On 21 August Monty wrote to General Sir Oliver Leese, then commanding the Eighth Army in Italy:

I have had to get rid of a few people you know. Bucknall could not manage a Corps once the battle became mobile, and I have Jorrocks [General Horrocks] in his place in 30 Corps. Bullen-Smith could do nothing with 51 Div so had to go; Thomas Rennie is there now and the Division is quite different under him. 7 Armd Div went right down and failed badly; so I removed Bobbie [Erskine] who had become very sticky, and put in Verney of the Guards Tank Brigade ...

On his arrival Horrocks assembled his staff in the corner of a walled orchard. The air was weighted with midsummer scents, wild flowers moving their white and scarlet heads in the breeze. Lush grass caressed our ankles. The sun cast shadows beneath the cap of the tall, loosely built General, standing like a figure of certainty in an uncertain theatre. His voice, strangely confiding in its huskiness, compelled attention. A man of paradox with a quick smile and steel-cold eyes, he was known to people who feared him as 'Death with a Smile'; humane, ruthless; humorous, single-minded; *bon viveur*, inflexible in duty. The man for the hour.

In the course of his address he gave us cold shivers by saying, 'We've got to get cracking. Tomorrow Corps HQ will move twenty miles forward, and the fighting formations will have to keep up with us!'

Afterwards he mingled with the officers, chatting informally. When he came to me he asked, 'Who are you?'

'Personal Assistant to the Chief of Staff, Sir.'

'Really? There's no provision for that on any establishment

I've ever heard of.'

Fearing that I might lose my job I told Pete what he had said.

'That's all right. I've spoken to Jorrocks – he knows I need you.'

I don't think we advanced as much as twenty miles, but we certainly moved forward a considerable distance the next day. There was already a new feeling in the Corps, rather like that experienced in the Eighth Army in the desert when Monty first took over, a feeling of purpose, of confidence.

Almost immediately steps were taken to reduce Villers Bocage. One evening we watched wave after wave of Lancaster bombers attack it. Aunay-sur-Odon received the same treat-ment. The great aircraft approached like a swarm of bees, not in any formation such as the USAF used for their carpet-bombing of towns. At intervals a single plane, or a small group of them, would swoop down from the circling swarm and dive at a given target.

At the time the attack seemed totally successful. Later we learned that very few Germans had been killed, having withdrawn quickly in their vehicles when the raid started, but casualties among civilians were horrifying in their proportions.

Furthermore, the destruction was so great that it took three days to clear passages through the ruins so that our troops could pursue the enemy. Eventually Pete and I set off in the jeep to scrape a way through Villers Bocage. This was a scorching summer. There was no wind in the shattered streets, so the stench of corpses rotting under the rubble became intolerable. Bile rose in determined gushes up my throat and I knew that at any moment I would vomit, a performance that would not appeal to Pete. Hastily I dabbed some Dettol from the First Aid kit onto my handkerchief and applied it to my nose and mouth. Even this did not quell the hawking noises as I swallowed the bile back.

'Really, Peter,' Pete said contemptuously, 'You certainly are an amateur soldier, aren't you!'

Not trusting myself to speak I nodded humbly and put my foot on the accelerator, steering dangerously with one hand, hoping to reach an open space before unloading myself in such an embarrassing way.

Soon the great battles of Falaise and Caen were to take

place. We broke out of Normandy, crossed the Seine at Vernon and headed north towards Belgium. We passed through, or near, places made famous in the Great War: Amiens, the Vimy Ridge, Tournai, Arras, Mons. Glimpses of huge white-crossed cemeteries raised doubts about the usefulness of wars. What had all those men died for? They thought theirs was a war to end wars, yet here were we, victims of yet another carnage, advancing over the same ground, facing the same enemy. Better, in these circumstances, to turn away from those reminders of futile sacrifice and concentrate on the matter in hand; such thoughts lead too directly to hopelessness. There would be time for that later, after the victory parades and rejoicings, when life must be met without drama. That is, of course, if one is still alive and in one piece.

Brussels – September 1944

I was seated in the wireless van at the Duty Staff Officer's desk, one hand holding a pencil and the other pressing the phone to my ear. Opposite me the Signal Corps Sergeant was desperately trying to adjust the set. An important message was coming in from 11th Armoured Division at Antwerp, and reception was bad. For an hour we had struggled to receive accurately, but interference from overhead power lines proved almost too much, and Division was becoming impatient.

Dawn was near. For over a week we had not slept, firstly because the advance through Belgium had been so rapid, and secondly because the welcome given to us by the citizens of Brussels had been so tumultuous, so ecstatic, that the celebrations turned night into day. Never had such passions been let loose at the liberation of a city, and to indulge in such a mundane occupation as sleep would be to miss history in the making.

Worn out with fatigue and excitement we forced our attention onto mastering the reluctant wireless waves. Corps HQ was in the grounds of the Château de Laeken, the residence of the Royal Family, and the stillness of the gardens contrasted with our furious activity and the weird, insistent noises captured by the set and flung into our tortured ears. At last, however, the full text was down, checked and acknowledged. The Sergeant mopped his brow and fell forward on the desk, fast asleep, his earphones on his head.

I leaned back in my chair, lit a cigarette to keep me awake, and let the events of the past few days flit across my mind like a newsreel. On the morning of 4 September, when Corps HQ entered the suburbs in convoy, the people climbed upon the vehicles, shouting and garlanding us with flowers, handing out bottles of wine and slabs of chocolate. As we neared the centre of the city the crowds became denser, wilder, more hysterical in their joy, and eventually the convoy was forced to a halt.

As usual I was driving Pete's jeep. Naturally he was impatient at the delay, since it was imperative that we should not lose touch with the fighting units that had already passed through Brussels. The crowd, like a relentless tide, flowed around and over us. Girls embraced us and mothers thrust forward their babies to be kissed. Breaking off a rather damp and lengthy bout of baby-kissing I turned to see how Pete was getting on. Behold, it was no brigadier who was seated beside me, but a blonde, a luscious, lovely blonde! She smiled and hugged me vigorously. The crowd cheered and I have to confess that I made little effort to extricate myself until I heard a familiar voice.

'Well, well, Peter, you seem to be busy!'

'Yes, Sir,' I replied, wriggling free and wiping the lipstick off my mouth. 'I thought you'd been kidnapped.'

'You seemed very worried about it, I must say. I've been up to the front of the column to find out what the delay is. All these damned civilians blocking the road. We *must* move on – there's work to be done. Ah! The column's moving – tell this young lady to get out of my seat, please.'

He was too busy to say it himself, so I translated. She obeyed, but not as he had intended. She vacated the passenger's seat by moving over towards me, sitting on my greatcoat, which was folded between the seats. By now the vehicle in front had moved on, so he had no choice but to jump aboard. At once Linette put one arm round my shoulders and one round Pete's. Above the cheering of the crowd ribald remarks could be heard from the men in the armoured car behind us. Pete, who had a fine sense of his own dignity, told me to order her to remove her arm. She did so, but first planted a smacking kiss on his cheek.

'Why does he look so cross?' she asked. 'Does he not like being kissed? Perhaps he has drunk too much champagne and his head hurts.' She looked indignantly at the man who scorned her beauty.

'What's she saying?' asked Pete abstractedly, conscious that he was the subject of conversation.

'She's admiring your ribbons, Sir. She says you must be a very brave man.'

Linette continued: 'Anyway he's an ugly old toad. I don't care whether he wants me to kiss him or not!'

Pete raised his eyebrows.

'She says she's most honoured to be sitting beside a general, Sir, especially such a handsome one.'

He softened. 'Tell her I'll give her my autograph,' he said, and patted her knee.

'I don't want his bloody autograph,' seethed Linette, who understood a few words of English, 'and tell him to keep his hands to himself!'

'Please!' I remonstrated, 'Please accept his autograph. It will be very hard for me if you don't!'

'He is cruel too? Then for your sake I will have it.' She burrowed in her handbag and produced a scrap of paper. With a fine flourish Pete wrote his name. He smiled coyly.

'Seems I've made a bit of a conquest, eh, Peter!'

Later that day I was granted a few hours' leave and drove round to visit Linette's family, who owned a beauty parlour near the Avenue Princesse Louise. I was told to look out for a shop called Ollywood.

On arrival I found the whole family paraded to meet me. Grandpapa was a magnificent, erect veteran who had fought in 1870 and 1914, and in this war acted as an intelligence offi-cer for La Brigade Blanche, the Belgian forces of the Resistance. He fell on my neck and, tears streaming down his beard, welcomed me as though I were his prodigal son. Grand'maman, equally charming, equally lachrymose, also embraced me. Papa, squat, shrewd, humorous, heavy-jawed, known to his family as 'Musso' on account of his likeness to that celebrity; Maman, gracious and handsome; Monique, the elder and married sister, a dark version of Linette – each took a turn, followed by miscellaneous aunts and cousins. Finally, Linette assailed me, a treat somewhat diluted by the fact that Papa photographed the scene with his Ciné Kodak. Such moments should be allowed to pass away into the unreality where they properly belong. I had a vision of the cynical smile that would cross my wife's face if she ever saw the film, and of myself spinning the unconvincing story.

We entered the living-room, where a long table was set gallantly for a meal, despite the shortage of rations. Before we reached this, however, there was an obstacle to be overcome: another, smaller table, laden with bottles of champagne and cognac.

We drank toasts. My hosts raised their glasses to The Liberators. I replied with The Belgians. Then they drank to Me. I equalized with My Hosts. They went ahead with My Family. I drew level with Les Bruxellois. They scored heavily with His Majesty King George VI. I came back limply with The Regent. They increased their lead with The Royal Tank Regiment. I caught up briskly with La Brigade Blanche. Then someone asked me to explain my ribbons. The first being a paltry decoration they drank to Le Héro; I returned, gracefully it seemed to me, with Tous les Héros Belgiques. When they discovered that my next ribbon was the Africa Star (Eighth Army clasp) there was a shout of glee, and we all drank to the Eighth Army. This put them one up and I racked my brains for a toast to make us all square. All I could think of was Le Mannequin Pisse, but I felt I didn't yet know them well enough. At last, amid an expectant hush, I raised my glass, 'A vous, mes amis courageux, les vrais vainqueurs de la guerre!'

'Charmant,' murmured Maman, flinging her arms round my neck and giving me a resounding kiss. I saw that the remainder of the family were preparing to follow her example. Steadying myself, I received the osculatory homage of the entire tribe once more.

As Monique released me there was a cough near the door. A young man was standing there, a young man of terrible aspect, his head in a bandage, his eyes bloodshot, two revolvers and three hand-grenades hanging loosely from his belt.

'Alphonse!' shouted Monique, rushing forward and kissing him with passion, the while passing her hands tenderly over his wounded head. She cooed her apprehension and he answered in abrupt monosyllables as he kept a steely and hostile eye on me.

'Mon mari,' explained Monique. 'He has been hunting Boches in the woods.'

Alphonse continued to stare at me, until I began to feel that I was indeed the sort of chap who did nothing but drink champagne and make love to the wives of men who hunted Boches in the woods. To relieve this situation I picked up my glass (now mysteriously replenished) and cried: 'Vive La Brigade Blanche!'

'Huzzah!' everyone shouted, 'La Brigade Blanche!'

'La Huitième Armée!' chimed in Grandpapa, whose age and deafness made him unaware that we had already played this tune.

Alphonse belched loudly and was led away amid the shocked vituperations of his in-laws. The champagne was by now finished, so we settled down to eat. The meal, accompanied by tumblerfuls of cognac, was a decided success, especially as at intervals Alphonse would appear waving a hand-grenade more or less in my direction, and utter a few remarkable oaths before being hustled away by his female relatives.

He needed rest, they explained. He had killed fifteen Boches in the woods this morning – no need to take prisoners now – and after a drink or two in the suburbs had driven his car head-on into a lamppost in the city. Well, it wasn't his car, it belonged to the authorities, so that was all right. Unfortunately, his passenger had been killed. But in war many men are killed, indeed *c'est la guerre*, and one must not let such trivial happenings interfere with celebrating *La Libération*. Poor Alphonse, he was suffering from shock, but he'd be all right in the morning. The problem was what would he do with himself now that there were no more Boches to be killed in the woods.

During the meal I was told about the Gestapo. For the last six months they had been looking for young people to take to Germany as labour replacements for men required in the fighting services. Their method of recruiting was simple: they apprehended in the streets anyone below the age of twenty-one. As a result the young people remained indoors, an ordeal which usually caused psychological distress after a few months. To combat this going to ground, the Gestapo instituted house-to-house searches. Being Germans, and therefore methodical, they began their searches at one end of the street and worked along, knocking noisily on each door.

Afterwards my friends showed me a false door in their kitchen which led into their neighbours' basement. There were young people next door too, but whichever of the two houses the Gestapo were searching, their quarry was in the other.

The kitchen was small, neat and excellently appointed, as is the way on the Continent. With housewifely pride my hostess pointed out her meat-safe. I politely made the right comments, though I am never normally inspired to go into ecstasies over the beauties of meat-safes. She bade me open it, which I did. She asked me if I noticed anything remarkable about it, which I didn't. Except, I added hastily to save face, that it was empty, which was understandable ...

Empty!

The whole family rocked with laughter. Papa then put his hand inside, palm upward, gave the ceiling a slight push upward and to one side, slipped it skilfully out of the door and there, lo and behold, was a radio!

'We used to listen to the Eighth Army news bulletins every night from the BBC. After the great victory of El Alamein the words Eighth Army were synonymous with us for hope. Vive La Huitième Armée!'

We trooped upstairs to see if there were anything left in the bottles to drink again to La Huitième Armée. Grandpapa was looking a little bewildered.

That had all happened a few days ago, and now here I was sitting tired and dry-mouthed in the wireless vehicle. A deep chill was creeping over my body, the chill of dawn and of exhaustion. The Sergeant had momentarily wakened and placed his greatcoat over his shoulders. He was snoring slightly. In half an hour I must wake him and sleep myself. There was no traffic on the air now.

I heard voices outside. Some sort of conference seemed to be going on and I caught the words 'Duty Officer'. Shaking myself fully awake, I opened the door; the lights in the vehicle automatically switched off.

It was less dark outside than I had expected. The trees were black in the scant light and a white mist lay on the ground like a carpet. The officer on the step identified himself.

'Captain Castle, Intelligence Officer, 11th Armoured Division.'

'Castle! Good God, man, haven't seen you since OCTU! Come on in!'

We had been cadets in the same troop but, because of a difference in temperament as well as in interests, had never been more than friendly associates, and so had not kept up with each other. Now we sketched in the gaps in our respective experiences since those distant-seeming days on Salisbury Plain, discussed the present tactical situation with learned fervour, and dwelt on the astonishing times and places fate chose for rendezvous. He had a rather pompous but not unpleasant way of talking, as though he were listening to himself making a recording and quietly appreciating his own turn of phrase. For a moment I found it hard not to smile as he embarked on his description of the Antwerp battle.

'Your regiment played the leading part.' This was the 3rd Battalion, the Royal Tank Regiment.

'You would see a tank standing at a street corner laden with lovelies, flowers and bottles of vino. When the commander gave the word the girls scrambled off and the tank, still girt with horticulture, drove round the corner, loosed off half a dozen rounds or so, and then reversed to its original position. The girls, screaming with love and laughter, scrambled on board again. It was a kind of ghastly carnival, a macabre Battle of Flowers. Which reminds me, the general commanding Antwerp Garrison – his name is von Stolberg-Stolberg – was captured last night. I've got him outside. He wants to see your general.'

'Our general isn't very keen on entertaining German generals, especially at five in the morning. What do you think we'd better do? We can't have him in here.'

'I don't know. He's not in a very good temper. He's offended at being given only a captain to escort him – and he'll be even more furious now that we've kept him hanging about in the cold light of dawn!'

'I'll go and see the Chief of Staff.'

On the way to Pete's caravan we passed the General, a tall, gaunt, bare-headed figure, his hands deep in his greatcoat pockets, who kept his head averted, even when we approached. He reminded me of one of those statues in grey stone that adorn the grounds of ancient palaces, remote and still, the distinguished nonentities of another age.

Pete told me to take him down to the officers' mess and give him some breakfast.

'What if the orderlies refuse to serve him, Sir? You remember they wouldn't serve that SS colonel we picked up in Normandy.'

'You can't force them, they've every right to refuse to serve a German if they wish. But he is a general officer – hm – would you mind serving him yourself?'

'No, Sir. But *he* might when he sees my cooking! What shall I say to him about seeing our general?'

'Tell him we're not fighting this war for the pleasure of entertaining German generals – he's lucky to be allowed to eat in the officers' mess. The Corps Commander is far too busy to waste time chatting with every bloody Hun we collect. Our friend will be on his way back to Army HQ in a couple of hours.'

'Thanks, Sir. Sorry to have wakened you.'

'That's all right, but don't do it again – not even if you get Hitler!'

I returned to Castle with my instructions. Knowing little German I had to rely on his interpreting. Von Stolberg-Stolberg scowled, but consented to accompany us to the mess tent.

The servants were not enthusiastic but did grumblingly agree to serve breakfast. While we waited I swept a clearing among the empty champagne bottles that littered the table like a bank holiday crowd on Margate beach. The General looked with disdain at this evidence of British military decadence.

Castle and I continued our conversation. The General, sitting opposite us in the deepest depression, stared at the middle of the table, immobile. I was beginning to enjoy myself, laughing loudly at one of Castle's anecdotes, when the General sharply interrupted us.

'What did he say?' I asked.

'He wants to know if it is usual for junior officers in the British Army to laugh and joke in the presence of a general officer.'

'My God, does he really? Tell him that if he doesn't like us he should be more careful not to be taken prisoner in future.'

Von Stolberg-Stolberg sat up stiffly when Castle translated and glared blackly at me. Uncomfortably I had to match his stare until at last he shrugged and resumed his broken attitude, his eyes fixed on the middle of the table.

'Tell me more about Antwerp,' I said to Castle.

He continued, and as he spoke I was aware that the General was intently trying to follow what he said. Castle was illustrating the tactical battle with champagne bottles and cutlery. He had reached the point where the tanks entered the city when I remarked how extraordinary it was that the Germans seemed to have been taken by surprise. After all, there was only one approach, and that afforded no cover.

'Ask His Highness here how it happened.'

The reply was instantaneous and explosive, Castle translating at intervals when he got the opportunity.

'First, the British arrived three days before I was told to expect them. Then they brought tanks up the road in broad daylight! My defensive positions were perfect.' Here he seized Castle's champagne bottles and proceeded to lay out the plan of his dispositions. His face was no longer bleak, but sharp and animated. He forgot that his audience was so junior; he was now the professional soldier absorbed in fighting the battle over again.

'Here is the river, here is the anti-tank ditch, here is my anti-tank gun screen. Perfect field of fire, perfect cover. The British tanks came straight up the main road – would you believe such stupidity! and drove into the city. Nobody but a fool would invest a city with tanks. Street fighting is the work of infantry, not tanks! Nobody but a fool – '

Acidly Castle cut him short: 'Nevertheless, General, that fool is now commanding Antwerp Garrison.'

The General stared at him haughtily. There followed a hostile silence, disturbed only by the sound of our breathing and the background clatter of dishes being prepared. In silence we sat on, a still miniature of the bitterness of defeat face to face with victory. Von Stolberg-Stolberg could not yet adjust himself to the humiliation of his position. He was no bumped-up Nazi, but a Prussian aristocrat playing the game according to the rules. These rules had been broken, first by the British tank commander who had apparently read a different manual of armoured warfare and, secondly and more personally, by our corps commander, who had insolently committed him to the care of a couple of captains and refused to meet him. Tradition dies hard, and it dies hardest for its slaves.

The Mess Sergeant entered, followed by his minions.

'Breakfast is ready, Sir. Shall I serve it?'

I nodded.

The pace was fast as we drove north again, the road lined with exultant troops, their triumph contrasting with the number of burnt-out vehicles at the side. We halted in the main street of a village and the cooks prepared a hot meal for us, which I decided to eat at the back of a lorry in the sun.

As I speared the sausages with deliberation, savouring every morsel, I heard rather than saw a movement in front of me, and looked up at a semicircle of some twenty children. Their eyes were fixed upon my plate, longingly, to the exclusion of all other sensation, saliva drooling from their lips, their noses wrinkled up at the rich smell. Realizing that they were almost starving, a great pity came over me. What should I do? Give the few remaining mouthfuls to perhaps two or three kids and thereby exacerbate the hunger of the others? Certainly I couldn't go on eating in front of them. With a sickening sense of betrayal I walked to the other end of the vehicle, where, unseen by the children, I shovelled what was left into my mouth. Even the sausages were now utterly tasteless.

I went over to the cooks' vehicle and asked if they could spare anything for the children.

'Sir, it's 'orrible to see them,' the Sergeant replied, 'but what can we do? If we feed some of them dozens more will come out. We just 'aven't the rations to go round. And if our own blokes 'aven't enough to eat, we can't go on liberating, can we?'

I saw the logic of what he said, and I must admit that a heaviness lifted from my heart as the column moved on again and I no longer had to face those pathetic little waifs.

On Tuesday 19 September we moved out of our leaguer on the heath south of Bourg Léopold at about 1640 hours. The trees were dank, dark and heavily oppressive. Pete and I were now in a new scout car, which offered a little more protection

than the jeep, but at the expense of visibility. There was a sigh
of relief when we were across 'Joe's Bridge' (Meuse-Escaut
Canal), as it had been bombed the previous night. 'Joe' was Lt-
Col J.O.E. Vandaleur DSO, 3rd Battalion, Irish Armoured
Guards, who on 10 September brilliantly captured a small
bridgehead on the northern bank of the canal. This was of great
tactical advantage to Dempsey, commanding the Second
Army, as he needed the canal bridge to continue his advance
against a heavily defended position.

It was nearly dark before we reached Valkensward. Belgium
was now behind us, and the liberation of Holland well under
way. The column was progressing very slowly, not more than
two miles an hour. Pete and I 'swanned' ahead time and time
again to get it moving. The chief trouble was that the drivers
were falling asleep at halts and not noticing that the vehicle in
front had gone on.

There was a great deal of activity ahead of us but we could
not make out what was happening. Then Bill Nolan, our brilliant GSO 2, Intelligence, turned up and told us that Eindhoven,
about seven miles north, had been badly bombed. By now we
could see the flames against the darkening sky. Several ammo
and petrol lorries had been hit. Some drivers panicked, and,
trying to escape, blocked the road against the oncoming
column. Fortunately, equilibrium was restored by the superb
behaviour of the US parachute troops, aided by local civilians,
who directed the traffic through a new diversion.

When we reached Eindhoven at 0500 hours there was a
terrific traffic jam, with vehicles and tanks three abreast. It was
decided that we should halt until first light. Utterly exhausted I
lay down on the engine cowling of the car, insensible to the
drizzling rain and the steel surface, and fell asleep.

We moved off again at 0630 hours. Refreshed, I responded
with deep emotion to the cheers of the people who had come
out to greet us in the cold, wet dawn. The bomb damage was
horrible. Hardly a pane of glass was left intact in the whole
town. Houses gaped where walls had collapsed, often revealing
the insignia of intimate home life, a nightdress draped across a
tilting bed, a bathroom with water spouting over a broken
basin, a table laid for a breakfast no one would eat. The sight of
fifteen burnt-out RASC lorries in one street was a grim

reminder that we were the real targets, and would continue to be shot at long after we'd left the gutted, liberated towns, where at least something like normal living could be restored.

Bill, who had interviewed the manager, told me that most of Philips Radio Works had been destroyed. Before the war 17,000 workers were employed there. So important were these works to the Germans that they stepped this up to 23,000. Production fell to 25 per cent.

We set off again, led by the 44 RTR. The idea was to rush the Zon Bridge, but the arrival of some Panther tanks made this too costly. Orders came to 'freeze' Corps HQ for a while. I took advantage of this to visit a small and very clean barber's shop. A shave and a wash and a chat in pidgin English-Dutch with the proprietor relaxed me greatly. Money was no use to him, but his gratitude for a packet of cigarettes was embarrassing.

In a tidy little battle three enemy tanks were knocked out and their infantry demoralized by 44 RTR, who had deployed to the right beyond the town in a clever manoeuvre.

Driving towards St Oedenrode we passed a column of prisoners, taken by the US Airborne troops. There was an air of total dejection, accentuated by the standard grey greatcoats, now creased and caked with mud and blood. Most of the men stared at the ground, some of the younger ones glancing at us in curiosity as we swept past. In field after field we saw the grounded American gliders, great unwieldy flimsy things, suggesting the wooden horse of the Greeks at Troy.

At St Oedenrode we received a wonderful welcome, the population excitedly telling us of 100 enemy tanks deployed in nearby woods, and thousands of infantry. Pete remarked that according to local rumours we must have passed more tanks and infantry than existed in the whole German Army. It was a dry comment, but he would have been the first to acknowledge the tremendous help we got from the Resistance groups in France, Belgium and Holland, and the general accuracy of their intelligence reports when they came to us directly from the fighters involved.

Looking back, the mind is conscious of the terrific urgency to reach Arnhem quickly. At the time, one was aware that this was our driving force, yet scenes of the immediate surroundings are photographed, static, in the memory. We pushed on through Veghel to Graves, and crossed that great nine-span bridge on the river Maas. Hundreds of people, all wheeling bikes, lined the road. As Pete and I watched the column of tanks and troops pass, we saw about fifty Stirling bombers flying towards us, very low. For one sickening moment it seemed they had mistaken us for enemy. Suddenly a blaze of colours exploded beneath them as thousands of blue and orange parachutes opened and fell slowly earthwards. We watched three flights of these airborne supplies dropping, and two more were to follow later.

By now it was becoming clear that after the initial euphoria of the airborne landings at Arnhem, and what had appeared the sheer brilliance of the operation, the 1st British Airborne Division had run into difficulties and were crying out for reinforcements. Communications were bad due to appalling weather and the heavy bombardment, and it was impossible to know what was really happening.

Forward we pushed, eyes smarting from the dust which permeated everything, itching down one's neck, caking on sweating hands, inducing a feeling of filth, unlike the clean sand of the desert.

On 29 September we received two very different pieces of news. The happy one was that Pete had been made a CBE. His excitement was delightful, revealing that under the stern guise of the professional soldier there was still a boyishness, transparent in his joy at being recognized and publicly rewarded.

Against this came news that David Silvertop, who had commanded 3 RTR so well in the desert and subsequently, had been killed. When I was his adjutant we clashed on so many points that it was a relief when I resigned the post. But I remembered my shock when he was so badly wounded in North Africa that Father Joyce had given him the last rites. Through sheer courage he had overcome his wounds and returned to command us. When the battalion played so great a part in the liberation of Antwerp the citizens renamed a street in his honour.

Much has been written of the race to capture the bridges across the rivers Waal and Neder-Rhine. This is no more than a brief personal account.

We moved into the village of Wijchen, about a mile from

Nijmegen. The operations room and the administrative offices
were set up in the school buildings of a nunnery, a place of
peace and beauty. The GOC and Pete established their HQs in
the spacious walled garden. My penthouse looked straight
onto the front door. It was moving to see these old nuns going
on with their daily chores despite the invasion of a crowd of
military males. We saw them drawing water, haggling with
the milkman, receiving poor people who came to them for
vegetables; and several times a day they trooped out of the
chapel after service, averting their eyes from the little privies
we had built in the orchard.

I noted in my diary, 'I can't say I see a wonderful religious
light in their eyes, but maybe I'm blind to that sort of thing. I
get the impression of rather sad, disappointed, even warped
faces. There is no spring in their step.'

In my youthful insensitivity I overlooked the courage with
which these nuns had borne the Occupation, continuing to
serve their community with devotion. It was little wonder that
they looked sad and had no spring in their step.

I now began to feel restless. Fully recovered from my wounds,
my job of personal assistant to Pete was becoming too restric-
tive for my new-found energy. I asked him if he would release
me and let me return to my battalion, the 3 RTR, whom I had
visited recently, feeling again the pull of their camaraderie.

Pete understood, advising me to be patient. Then one day
he called me into his caravan and said, 'Your posting has come
through. A jeep will be put at your disposal to take you to the
coast. You will have a fortnight's leave and then report to
Sandhurst as an instructor.'

'Sir, I'd hoped to rejoin the battalion.'

'Yes, yes, I know. But your last experience of battle was in
the desert – very different from where we are now. With all the
will in the world you'd never catch up, you'd only be a
liability. But you've a lot to offer as an instructor, especially at
Sandhurst, which is an RAC OCTU now.'

So I reverted to type, becoming a schoolmaster again.

Sandhurst

My time at Sandhurst was happy. We rented a small house in
Camberley and settled down in a home of our own for the first

time in our married life. Our baby son, David, was then aged four months.

I was appointed administrative officer to C Squadron, my squadron leader being Ronnie Aird MC, Secretary of the MCC, one of the pleasantest men I have ever served under. I acted as his second-in-command and adjutant.

Ronnie ran his squadron on a very simple maxim: 'People work much better and are far more efficient when they are happy.' He had a fundamental sincerity and strength of purpose which made it impossible for anyone to mistake what he meant by happiness. He did not mean flippancy. He meant that where a group of people take pleasure in their work, and work as a team, where they know they will always be treated with the utmost fairness and consideration and not as mere cyphers, where they feel confident they can approach their officers on any matter under the sun, however personal, and be met with sympathy, then the members of that group are already more than half-way to success. Results proved him right.

Unfortunately there is a cast of military mind in some officers which takes a poor view of such flexibility. These are the 'Blimps', men who know and love their job but, fearing that deviation may lead to chaos, have not the confidence to depart from the rules. Among these Ronnie was very suspect. It never occurred to them to examine his methods or his results.

This disapproval once nearly cost Ronnie his command. Had he been a regular soldier further promotion would have been unlikely, but it was a matter of weeks before his demobilization, so he was tolerated.

The occasion was a TEWT (Tactical Exercise Without Troops) which was taking place in an area a few miles from Sandhurst. Some very senior officers were present as observers. The RV was a hill behind a large farm. All were there at the appointed time except Ronnie. As his second-in-command I was embarrassed both by his failure to turn up and by the derogatory comments of some officers: 'Typical of these temporary officers – need discipline.' As we waited, a huge flock of sheep appeared from the farmyard and moved raggedly towards us up the hill. In their midst was Ronnie, weaving through in his jeep, slapping their backsides and singing with great abandon a popular song of the time, 'Mares e doats and hares e doats and little lambs e divy ...'

When he saw the assembled Brass he stood up to salute. His driver chose that moment to swerve past a particularly large sheep, and Ronnie pitched head first into the mire, emerging covered with dung, grinning and saluting superbly.

The cadets' final day at Sandhurst was always a Saturday. After an address by the Commandant there was a Passing Out Parade, attending by friends and relatives. After the Inspecting General's speech they marched, in slow time, to the strains of 'Auld Lang Syne', up the impressive steps and into the Old Building. The Adjutant, mounted on a white horse, followed them up the steps. As soon as they had disappeared the band played 'There'll always be an England', and a new troop, which had entered the OCTU the day before, marched onto the parade-ground and halted where the passing out troop had stood. It was a moving ceremony, watching all these young men at their physical and intellectual peaks, and wondering how many of them would be alive in six months' time.

In the evening there was a Passing Out Dinner to which the cadets invited the Commandant, the Adjutant, their squadron leader, the chief instructors, and all the officers who had trained them. As the war drew towards an end the intake of cadets was slowed down. The OCTU was to be reduced to two squadrons, A and B. The others, C, HAC (for armoured car training), D, and E (for the Reconnaissance Regiment), were to be closed down in reverse order.

When HAC was closed I realized with horror that we were next on the list. Ronnie would be gone and I would become junior officer in B Squadron, not a pleasant prospect after my stint as second-in-command of C Squadron, running it while Ronnie concerned himself with the affairs of the MCC.

I made a decision. The Commandant, Colonel W.H. Hutton DSO, MC, granted my request for an interview. It went something like this.

'Yes?'

'Sir, I think a book should be written about the history of Sandhurst during the war.'

'Good idea. Who do you think should write it?'

'Me, Sir.'

'What qualifications have *you* got?'

'Well, Sir, I've published a lot of articles and book reviews' –
this was something of an exaggeration – 'and I have a First
Class Honors degree in English' – which was not really a
qualification at all.

He seemed interested and said he would put it up to
Authority.

A few weeks later I was told to go ahead. A limit was set on
the length of the book because paper was scarce at the time. I
was given a room in the College Library, the typing services of
the office staff, leave to visit the War Office when research
made it necessary, and the help of a brilliant artist, Captain
G.D. Machin DFC, illustrator to MT Directorate, the War Office.
I had three months in which to do the job and would receive
staff pay. *To the Stars* was published in 1946, my first book.

In this way my military service drew to a close. It ended as I
would have wished, with an act of creativity.